About the Author

Phil Avery lives outside Cambridge with his wife and their two dogs. He has worked variously as a Civil Engineer, University Lecturer, Construction Contracts Manager and Mathematics Teacher over his career.

Windmills of my Mind

Phil Avery

Windmills of my Mind

Vanguard Press

VANGUARD PAPERBACK

© Copyright 2024
Phil Avery

A CIP catalogue record for this title is
available from the British Library.

ISBN 978 1 80016 937 1

This is a work of creative non-fiction. The events are portrayed to the best of
the author's memory. While some of the stories in this book are true, names
and identifying details have been changed to protect the privacy of the people
involved.

Vanguard Press is an imprint of
Pegasus Elliot Mackenzie Publishers Ltd.
www.pegasuspublishers.com

First Published in 2024

Vanguard Press
Sheraton House Castle Park
Cambridge England

Printed & Bound in Great Britain

To the ones I love and who love me.

Chapter 1

"Tell us a joke, sir."

It always seemed to start like this. I knew it was their way of delaying the start of the lesson as Construction Technology was not that fascinating for them. I said 'lesson' but that suggests visions of schools, perhaps 'lecture' may have been more appropriate but that conjures images of university. These sixteen-to seventeen-year-old lads had enrolled on a technicians course at a further education college as part of their full time education up to the age of eighteen. The college is on the outskirts of Lincoln, a dreary establishment in rural Lincolnshire. No one wanted to be there it seemed, and sadly, I was slipping into that category too.

"You're the joke, Ben," I retorted.

"Oh, very funny," was the obvious reply.

The pile of paper handouts sitting on the desk waiting to be perused, consisted of piled foundation techniques and I had spent several hours getting sketches, diagrams, descriptions and applications ready for them.

"Let's start today by looking at flight auger drilling rigs," I said in the hope of triggering some interest.

"That's boring, sir."

"Actually, you're absolutely right, Ben."

"What about?"

And there was the joke.

***

Back in the staff room, a large open plan office space littered with various desks, shelves, cupboards, pinboards and filing cabinets. Each desk was crammed with a computer, books and a seemingly unnecessary number of papers balanced precariously. Central to each workspace was the parochial custodian of each individual chaos, of which I was yet another, working to fulfil some sense and purpose of the inevitable futility of it all. In truth, by four-thirty p.m. a lot of these workspaces were vacant as the occupants had decided that a trip to the golf driving range, shops, cafés or a stiff drink at home or pub was a better prospect.

I was writing references for the three or four of my twenty-four strong tutor group who had decided that if they were going to 'make it' in this mad world, then climbing to the top of the tree via a degree may result in more autonomy and self-worth. For the others it was a case of 'we'll be all right' as they expected to walk into some job or other without much trouble. They were probably right, if all else failed they could always play golf, go for coffee or visit bars for a few beers. Education seems to bring its own inevitable cycles.

I was pondering these thoughts while cycling home, it wasn't far, just three or four miles but those twenty minutes or so made a nice interlude from the frustrations at work and the impending frustrations at home. This particular evening was fine as the sky had filled with those light wispy clouds and taken on those beautiful hues of orange and crimson from the setting sun. These clouds had mysteriously filled the void of the beautiful blue sky earlier in the day. The heat had gone too, but that was perfect for me as the chilling air brought some relief and I could breathe it in. The Lincolnshire Wolds held their own spectacular beauty, and it was comforting to me. I was used to it, after all I had been born in this county forty-two years earlier, and apart from my time studying at Bristol had always lived here.

***

Opening the front door brought normality back into sharp and clear focus.

"Dad!" screamed Sebastian as he ran through the dining room and jumped up at me. I allowed myself to wonder how many times he may do this before he turns from the excitable five-year-old into his nemesis, his twelve-year-old brother Francis, whose greeting was much more subdued.

"Mum, was wondering how much longer you were going to be."

"Hello boys," I said. "How was school?"

Sebastian was enthused. "Good, we were Roman soldiers today."

Francis's response was reminiscent of my own. "Boring. Mum wants to serve dinner now."

Bella had already served dinner. She was only thinly hiding her frustrations when she said, "You're nearly an hour late, Phil." It was nearer twenty minutes after my normal time, but with Bella you learned not to draw reference to the exaggeration.

"Sorry, Donna, I wanted to finish the references for UCAS." Donna was my nickname for her. No one else called her that though and her mother didn't like me doing so. Even more reason to do it then.

Fish, broccoli and pasta for us two. Chicken nuggets, chips and peas for the boys. Sometimes I wanted to be five again.

After loading the dishwasher, I wanted to say how unhappy I was at college but the response would be predictable. We'd been there before. She worked hard as a part time PA in a law firm where confidentialities are always observed. Her belief was that I should keep my counsel too and her arguments were succinct, relevant and unequivocal. In her mind I had a good job, responsibility, respect, good pay, long holidays and a pension most would die for. Sorry, the expression 'die for' was not appropriate. I chuckled to myself that Ben might have thought that was a good joke and I might try to remember that for tomorrow.

**

The next day was more of the same, except I had to cycle to work in the rain, battling against the Westerly wind. I hated going to work in the rain and much preferred it, if it had to rain, on the way home instead. Bella had once again made the point that she had to take the boys to school before she could go to work. The problem with teaching is we are all driven by the clock and if I needed to start a lesson at nine a.m., I could hardly drop the boys off at eight forty-five before cycling to college (which, incidentally, is in the opposite direction from the boy's schools). This was not a relevant argument to Bella and one I was keen not to push too hard.

I said that it was a normal day, but as it happened it livened up quite dramatically after lunch. The morning was normal as I taught Engineering Mathematics and introduced the reluctant mass ahead of me to the beauty and complexity of Calculus, always a pleasure as I could draw reference to my all-time hero, Isaac Newton. The second session was Environmental Science and teaching the students how to find heat losses from buildings via U values for walls, roofs, etc. As I write this, I still find these studies captivating and I lived in the hope that my enthusiasm would ignite a flame of interest.

During the lunch-break, I was walking back from the canteen clutching a tuna sandwich and a yoghurt when two of my more responsible students, James and Ollie, stopped me to say there was a problem with Dan and Alex. Now, Dan and Alex were two of the students I was most concerned about as their apathy and non-participation was becoming an issue. James told me they were being sick in the loos outside the plumbing workshops. Firstly, they shouldn't have been over there, and secondly, why were they being sick? On entering the toilets, it was clear from the empty bottle of 'Jack Daniels' discarded on the floor, the sight of two prostrate legs sticking out from under the door of one of the cubicles and a deep moaning from another cubicle what the problem was. I tried to clear the vomit from the mouths of first, Dan and then Alex, with wet tissues while James and Ollie fetched the first aiders from reception. Both boys were conscious fortunately and I knew enough first aid to put them in the recovery position and they allowed me to do so without too much complaint.

Looking at my suit trousers one of them had also very neatly decorated my right leg with a potent orangey trail of sick which I swear was littered with diced carrots and peas all served up in a sauce of distinctive American whisky. For a moment I wanted to roll them onto their backs and throw cold water all over them. What sort of tutor would do that though? Instead, I talked calmly to them to keep them awake and found some old overalls as makeshift pillows. After the first aiders arrived I left, discarded the tuna sandwich and yoghurt in the bin as I had, unsurprisingly, lost my appetite. I really hoped it was still raining when I go home as I didn't have another change of clothing and it might wash out the offending stains from my suit trouser.

The phone calls I had to make to Dan's mum and dad did not go well.

His dad exploded. "What the hell are you doing allowing them to have alcohol at college?" I tried to explain, but he continued. "You are supposed to be in Loco Parentis, and you will hear more from me when I get the facts." His mother was more conciliatory and offered to come and pick him up. I was unable to reach Alex's parents as the call to them went straight to Ansaphone. We were instructed not to leave messages but talk directly to the parent in such sensitive cases. As it happened, Dan's mother agreed to take Alex home as well.

Obviously, we did not see the boys the next day, which was a Friday. The next Monday however, the two of them came to me looking very contrite and sheepish.

"Can we talk to you Mr Avery?" They used my name instead of the obligatory and cursory "sir." I led them to an empty teaching room.

"OK, boys. How are you feeling?"

"All right — now. We want to apologise for what happened on Thursday."

I persisted. "So, what triggered that behaviour?"

Alex responded. "It was a bet from the plumbing students that we couldn't drink whisky from the bottle like Americans do in films. What we didn't know was that they were not drinking but only pretended to do so."

"You nutters! So where did the booze come from?"

Neither of the boys wanted to admit to where it came from but much later, I heard from some of the others that Dan had smuggled it in from his dad's cocktail cabinet.

At moments like this, I always found the best policy is not to criticise but try to be honest and encouraging.

"Lads, let me tell you a true story that happened five or six years ago. One of my surveying students died from alcoholic poisoning when he was at a New Year's Eve party. He was bet twenty pounds that he couldn't drink a pint of scotch. He was already drunk at the time, well, you would be to do something so stupid and reckless. He did it but died overnight from alcoholic poisoning. He was eighteen."

Alex looked down at his shoes, but Dan looked me in the eye. I continued.

"What struck me most was every time I taught that group, my gaze went straight to that one empty chair in the room where that lad would have been sitting. I wonder how those other lads felt after they made the dare which resulted in their friend dying so pointlessly? They will have to live with their conscious reminding them forever more."

I swear Alex was crying. At least a tear had appeared, and Dan put his hand on his shoulder to apologise for his part.

"Look you two, you have your whole lives ahead of you. You can't change the past and you have to start from here. You know I will help as much as I can but it's a two-way street."

"Thanks sir, we will try harder," said Dan.

"What is going to happen to us now?" asked Alex.

I had to be honest and could promise nothing. "We will have to wait and see what the disciplinary board will say but I will speak up for you, fundamentally, you are good lads."

As they turned to go out of the room, I stopped them and made them 'high five' with me. They needed to know they had a real friend and not an adversary which is what I think they saw me as before. Another part of the establishment keeping them in line.

Dan's father was true to his word and wrote a vociferous and condemning letter to the college principal outlining my apparent failures to properly control the students under my care and education. The disciplinary procedure took several weeks to come to a hearing as statements were drawn from the students themselves and their parents, witnesses, myself and two of my colleagues, the unions and my head of department. The whole thing was totally overblown. I struggle to remember the details of the hearing but the unfairness of the whole sorry episode sticks. In short, I managed to save the boys from being expelled from the college, but I had to agree to enrol on a short course for providing extended pastoral care and was given a written warning.

***

A few weeks later, Bella and I had been invited to a Choral Society get together and met up with several of our friends from the singing group. It was some point during the evening, I allowed my frustrations from working at the college to overspill and I was waxing about the unfairness of the system, failing not only the students but the staff involved in their education. The BTEC courses, which were designed to give technician status had been dumbed down to the lowest common denominator. Less emphasis on exams and more emphasis on projects and continuous assessments. In effect, box ticking exercises.

I remember one case at a midland's college, the Materials Lecturer handed an Engineering Class A brick to a student hoping to see if he could recognise whether it was a Staffordshire Red or an Accrington Blue and possibly quote it's crushing strength.

The student looked at it from all angles, sniffed at it and replied, "It's a brick, sir."

After the inevitable giggles, the lecturer persisted. "Tell me more about it."

The reply was priceless. "To be honest, sir, I am only looking for a pass not a distinction!"

Perhaps this dumbing down is more extensive than we think. Even my students had penned the acronym GNVQ as 'Going Nowhere Very Quickly'.

But I am digressing, during this very pleasant evening amongst friends and convivial company, I had somehow overstepped the mark as my wife, Bella, quietly whispered in my ear. "You are getting boring."

My friends sympathised with my situation I am sure, but there is a time and place, and this was not it, especially as we were preparing for Handel's 'Messiah'.

***

When we arrived home, Bella and I allowed the babysitter to depart clutching her ten-pound note with a promise to do the same next week when the performance was going to be made. Sebastian was fast asleep, but Francis was still awake and on the iPad in his bed. It worried me about the time that boy was spending looking at a screen, especially so late at night, I was sure it was affecting his sleep patterns. As usual, Bella suggested that I was becoming depressive. Was she right? I started to question my own self. Our sex life had deteriorated but thought that was normal after two kids and a fifteen-year marriage. I took less interest in things that did fascinate me once before. My motorbike hadn't been out of the garage for three years. I hadn't painted the garden fence with preservative as I promised two years ago. The garden and lawn cutting had become a chore and I hadn't bothered to renew my season ticket to see The Imps at Lincoln City FC.

I thought I should reverse this process. In bed that night, I rolled over gently and kissed Bella's shoulder and propped myself up on one elbow to look at her.

"Are you OK?" she asked.

"Yes, are you?" I asked as my hand started to move over her to cup her breast.

"Oh, come on it's getting late, you surely don't want this now, you've had too much to drink."

"It's Sunday tomorrow, we can sleep in."

"Sebastian won't sleep in."

That was the killer punch and I resigned myself to more frustration. After laying down again she destroyed any other potential advances by adding. "Have you forgotten, you are meeting John at ten tomorrow morning?"

I had forgotten actually; John and I are friends from university days. He hails from Plymouth but is now settled in a village just North of Lincoln. We both studied Civil Engineering at Bristol and I went on to specialise in structures whereas, John is more into geotechnics and foundation design. I had forgotten we were going to Sleaford in the morning to do some setting out of a pair of semi-detached houses for a building friend of his. It is good for me, I think, to keep myself involved in industry. So many teachers and lecturers I have met have been in academia too long and lost contact with the 'real world'. I was continuing to do the odd bit of design work now and again for small to medium sized building companies, sole trading architects and other clients. Fortunately, I had not allowed my Professional Indemnity to lapse when I moved into full time education seven or eight years ago. I designed the odd steel beam here, roof structure there, carried out structural surveys, and well, anything that kept me involved.

After loading the surveying equipment into John's car boot, we set off to the site. While John was driving, I had the chance to talk man to man. Bella had suggested that we take Francis for a day out but the prospect of having a bored twelve-year-old running around on a building site was not sensible. Sadly, I knew that Bella would add another black mark against my 'poor' parenting skills. To be fair, Francis didn't want to go anyway but Sebastian would have jumped at the chance. In the event, I was relieved that I had an opportunity to discuss matters with John on our own.

It was me that started the ball rolling as I thought I could say anything to John without fear of any recrimination. It was the 'Jack Daniels' saga that started it and John was outraged that the college would have used me as a scapegoat.

"That's how it works in education," was my passive response. "Parents, kids and the college management are never to be blamed."

"Fuck that," was his attitude.

I continued in my defence. "Perhaps I should have been more attentive, after all I knew there was something troubling those lads."

"How the hell were you to know that a bottle had been smuggled in? Then, consumed secretly behind the workshops during break?"

I was thinking of a reply when John started up again. "You gave up your lunchtime, cleaned the lads up, made them a safe environment, contacted all the right authorities, including their parents…"

"Not Alex's though," I interrupted.

"You tried to do so but couldn't leave a message due to the college protocol and they hold you solely responsible. Fuck that." He added venomously for more gravitas.

He was right of course. Bella had thought it unjust but wanted me to move on and learn from it. I think her words were, "Just keep your head down and don't let it get to you." I liked to think she added the word 'sweetheart', but she hadn't.

The setting out work was quite tricky in the end as the two semis fitted rather snugly between an existing house gable wall and the council's highway boundary. The front facade of each house was slightly stepped back from each other to match the curve of the road. I liked working with John as there is no problem he isn't prepared to overcome in a practical sense. Mind you, he was hopeless at setting up a theodolite and I relished it. I tried to teach him, and he reminded me that he wasn't one of my "bloody students". Adding, "it's horses for courses." In other words, I do my part and he will do his. Fair enough.

I was keen for us to have a drink and a quick lunch afterwards as I knew Bella had taken the boys to her parents for dinner. I was keen to keep offloading too, although I knew it wasn't fair to burden John, as he had his own problems. His wife had had an affair with one of her co-workers. Well, actually it was two of her co-workers at the same time! I was trying to be delicate when I said 'affair' as it was actually a highly charged sexual romp in a motel. Sorry, this is too much information and I know John certainly did not want to talk about it.

We both had a pint of 'Poacher's' and I settled on lasagne, but I have no recollection what John ordered.

John started. "Look, Phil, if you are unhappy at the college, move on. After all you've been there four years."

"Seven," I corrected him.

"Bloody hell, it's definitely time to move on then." He finished his pint. "Another?"

"Yes, but I shall fall asleep this afternoon."

"So will I," he said and then ordered two more from the bar.

"OK, this is what I think," he said on his return. "You are a good teacher but wasted in that place. Your students like you — God only knows why because your jokes are rubbish and you take yourself too seriously — but if you want to stay teaching, find somewhere else."

"There's nowhere else that I can teach construction and you know that." I added lamely.

"Well, Lincoln isn't the only place in the known world, is it?"

That hurt. No, hurt is the wrong word. That frightened me, would be more apt. Bella and I are happy here, the kids like their schools, I feel comfortable teaching at the college, despite everything, our music society is here, Bella's family, my dad... The list went on in my head.

John dropped me off about half two in the afternoon and I put the surveying equipment back in the garage. He was keen to get off home and said he would BACS my fee when he gets paid from the builder. It was our normal procedure, and I would send an invoice over later. Often,

John had to remind me as I was not great at sending invoices out. Money was never a great incentive to me. I still warm to the thought that when I first started teaching, I remember clearly overhearing a student remarking to his mate that he 'really gets it now' after I had explained shear force and bending moment diagrams to them. It meant more to me than the pay advice envelope I picked up later that day.

Sunday evening is never a good time to start a serious discussion, but John's words had been re-bounding in my brain all day. Bella got back just after four and she was not pleased to see me asleep on the settee with the television showing the Chelsea v West Ham game to no one in particular. At least Francis was an ally on this occasion.

"Great," he said, footie!"

Mind you the attention span of any twelve-year-old isn't long and by half time he'd already gone out into the garden to annoy Sebastian.

"How were mum and dad?" I asked.

"Disappointed that you were not there too," was the curt reply, adding in a softer tone. "They're OK, thanks, apart from dad's sciatica. He's driving my mum mad."

"I'm sorry for your mum."

Her dad was not the most patient of people and I could imagine he would be difficult to deal with, especially with his ill health. I suspected that it wasn't just sciatica that he was suffering from, but also gout.

Bella was not that interested in what John, and I had been working on and it wasn't worth the effort to tell her.

My attention span was not much better than Francis as by halfway through the second period when Chelsea were 2-0 up, I turned it off and thought about doing some of the odd jobs around the place. They remained thoughts though as I did my usual paper pushing on my desk upstairs, answered a few emails and got my 'lesson planner' arranged for the next couple of days. I also fell into the normal trap of playing Backgammon on the computer to pass the time.

By seven p.m., Bella expected me to get Sebastian to bed, which I was always delighted to do as I enjoyed reading Farmyard Tales about Mrs Boot the farmer, and her two children, Poppy and Sam and their dog, Rusty. I was hoping we could read 'Barn on Fire' again, but Sebastian wanted 'Pig Gets Stuck'. I was wondering if he might read it to me and I could fall asleep after drinking two pints of 'Poacher's'.

Francis was too cool now to have a book at bedtime and besides, he was at the grand old age of twelve so he argued his bedtime should be two hours after Sebastian's. That didn't cut mustard with Bella, and he was dispatched shortly after eight p.m. His protestations lasted a good hour longer so he got his wish anyway.

Over some cheese, grapes and crackers I plucked up the courage and floated an idea that had been brewing to Bella. "I thought I might look for another job," was my opening gambit.

"Are you thinking of going back to work with John?" It was a clever assessment after today. She went on. "But you never really felt comfortable doing design all day and you moaned about not having much spare time."

She was a master manipulator I decided. I hadn't formulated any meaningful plan going forward but already some doors were being slammed shut.

"Well, I've been at the college far too long." It was weak but a statement of fact.

The door closing began.

"There are loads of your colleagues who have been there happily for far longer than you." Slam! "You are in a much better position for promotion from within." Slam! "You have a protected and generous pension scheme." Slam!

"We are settled here" — Slam! "You like teaching the students." Slam!

She was right with the last salvo. Time to wave the white flag. "You are right and perhaps I'm feeling, well, just a little fed up with it all."

"Look," she said softly, "things will get better."

She gently touched my arm and I thought, 'great, we'll have sex tonight!'

Chapter 2

"Tell us a joke, sir."

I was feeling frivolous that morning and I almost resigned myself to either staying or going. The thought was preposterous of course but it did mean I was thinking about it.

"OK lads. So, there is Adam and Eve in the Garden of Eden. Adam tells Eve that he is going fishing for their meal tonight. Adam returns very late; it is almost dusk, and Eve confronts him angrily. 'Where have you been?' 'I'm sorry,' he replied, 'I hadn't realised how late it had become.' Eve was not convinced and accused him of having an affair with another woman. Adam says that is ridiculous as she was the only woman in creation. Oh, yes, Eve thought, but that night when Adam was fast asleep, she very carefully counted all his ribs."

Stoney silence. The swirls of prairie grass were blowing across the classroom with an eeriness combined with a gentle breeze.

Had no one studied Genesis from the Old Testament? Had no one told them that God made woman from Adam's rib?

It was Ben, of course, who broke the silence.

"Was he wearing a ribbed condom, sir?"

***

The morning's lesson (or lecture if you will) was going to be on 'caissons and cofferdams' but ten minutes into the lesson we were interrupted by the departmental secretary.

"Can I talk to you outside, Mr Avery?"

"Ooooh," went all the lads. "What have you done wrong this time, sir?"

"Copy down the diagram from the board and I will give you the notes to go with it in a moment." Stupidly, I added. "You are in charge, Ben," as I walked into the corridor.

"Great, feet up then everyone!" shouted the newly promoted corporal.

Outside, Mrs Watson looked very serious and anxious. I did think 'What had I done wrong this time?'

She whispered. "I am so sorry to tell you this Phil, but Jerry Unwin died last night."

Jerry was one of my colleagues in his early fifties and he had been at the college for twenty or so years, taught structural mechanics, amongst other things and was a great inspiration to me when I first joined. There was no indication he had been unwell, and we saw him hale and hearty only last Friday. As it happens, hearty was the problem as he suffered a massive coronary in his sleep. Now, I had the unpleasant task to tell the students, cover his lessons and make whatever arrangements I needed to smooth over this tragedy. Tragedy was the right word, as the students loved Jerry. He had an infectious laugh, and his jokes were so much better than mine. I started to wonder who would inherit his stash of books and teaching materials, I could have them, his workspace was better than mine as it was next to the window and it had some great views over the countryside, I could swap. I could take over teaching mechanics...

I started to well up, tears were forming in the corner of my eye. I chastised myself for thinking so shallowly at this time and realised the enormity of the situation.

"Thank you, Mrs Watson, I will let the students know and I will look at Jerry's timetable and see what we can arrange." I turned to go back into the room where little or no work had been done.

"Have you been sacked, sir?"

"Does Mrs Watson fancy you, sir?"

Perhaps my face said it all, but for once they collectively and instinctively knew something terrible had happened. Silence swamped them, they sat still and with genuine concern, listened attentively.

"I am so sorry lads, Mr Unwin, passed away last night."

Although they knew and understood the words, it hadn't sunk in properly.

"What's going to happen to him?" said Tom without engaging his brain.

"Well, there will be a bloody funeral obviously," someone said.

Tom tried backtracking. "I meant, will they need to do checks on him or something?"

I said that in these situations of sudden and unexplained deaths, there would always be a post-mortem examination. Although it was only nine-thirty a.m., I took the whole group down to the canteen and bought them all drinks and snacks and we could talk about Jerry. If anyone questioned my professionalism by taking students out of class at that moment, I was ready for them and I would kill them with my own bare hands.

Of course, tragedies like this pass quite quickly and by the end of the week the timetables had been re-adjusted, lessons re-organised and it was all back to normal.

I didn't swap my workspace of course, but I knew Jerry would want me to have his books and teaching materials. We had some sort of unwritten understanding about this sort of thing. A lot of his books were duplicates of mine anyway, but he had a superb collection of BRE digests and British Standards, no one else was having them. I was going to miss our chats though in the staff rest area; his monstrous seventy foot putt to save par, his Honda 400 four motorbike, his time as a site manager for the construction of a bus station and a bridge over the railway, reminiscing about his holidays just outside Valencia and how his daughter was expecting his first grandchild (of course, sadly, he would never see).

Jerry once recounted how he was about to show some slides on steel fire protection to a group of GNVQ students. He told them to pay attention and started to pull the screen down over the whiteboard when the students all burst into fits of laughter. Puzzled, he turned around to see that somebody had crudely drawn an enormous erect penis on the screen complete with jets of ejaculate.

We went to the funeral naturally, as many from the department as possible, and surprisingly, several of the students, including Ben, Dan and Alex. In many respects these seventeen-year-olds were maturing in front of me. As I looked around the crematorium, it was disgraceful to see that no one from the college management team were there, except a token human resources girl who didn't even know him.

It was time to move on. I didn't want Mrs Watson's successor to tell a member of staff that Phil Avery died last night, while they were standing in the corridor of an FE college.

***

The next afternoon before I cycled home, I popped into the library to look at the Times Educational Supplement (TES). It was always a dangerous manoeuvre as anyone seen reading the TES is suspected of plotting an escape route to another teaching post. In this case they would be right. As it happened there were few jobs that applied to me unless I was looking for a sideways move. There were posts that could have been possible, such as course co-ordinator in construction. This was technically a head of department's role but by renaming it they could drop the pay scale dramatically and any 'muggins' falling for that trap would regret it later. College management and HR departments have some devious ways to suck you in.

The cycle ride home was dreary that night as the dark February air had a knack of wrapping you in the damp and cold. All these things were starting to strengthen my resolve and I needed to get Bella to come onside.

"Hi Dad," said Francis.

"Dad!" screamed Sebastian and jumped up onto my chest where fortunately I was able to catch him, discarding bags and cycle helmet on the floor.

Bella came out of the lounge, kissed me quickly on the lips and asked if I'd had a good day. "Yes and No" was my ambiguous answer, but it was accepted as rhetorical and no more was said about it.

Bella started telling me about the choral groups desire to try Mozart's *Cosi Fan Tutte* as their next production and trying to arrange the cathedral, or at least, a side chapel in which to perform. I was not a great singer but even I knew this would be a serious challenge and require lots of practice, besides I am not a great fan of opera and much prefer church music.

I said, "Perhaps I should call you 'Dora' instead of 'Donna' then!"

The joke was lost on her until I explained the character in the opera was 'Dorabella' not 'Donnabella'.

Her reply was fairly flat with no conviction. "Oh, I see, very clever."

I wanted to be close to Bella much more now. I think Jerry's death and his funeral, combined with my unease at work, plus all the other things going on had left me feeling rudderless. I needed her now, more than ever, and the boys, to give some reason and purpose to my life.

That night in bed after she put down her book and turned out the lights, I rolled into her and started to rub her back. Her smell was so familiar and comforting but I was surprised by her reaction.

"What do you want now?"

That was a bit of a cold water moment and I was taken aback. "I thought we could make love"

Her reply was still defensive. "Look, we only did it a couple of nights ago."

"Ten," I corrected.

"Who's counting? And why are you counting? Is this some sort of test?" Her pitch and volume started to increase, and this was no time for any escalation.

"I just thought…"

"You thought about yourself. What about what I might want?" Her tone had lowered to a veiled hiss.

"I'm sorry," I said.

"Look. I'm tired and want to sleep," she said with a finality that was hard to ignore.

The slight glow on the ceiling through the curtains from the street lights became a source of fascination for a while. I imagined it formed the outline of Chile, or Norway possibly. I then turned it into a rock fissure and wondered what plants may grow from it. My sleeplessness continued for some time later and by two a.m. I was still wide awake. I got up quietly and slipped into my study to look at some online pornography. Whatever else, it doesn't take the pain or loneliness away I can assure you. I slipped back into bed at about three a.m. but annoyingly, I had disturbed Bella.

"Where have you been?" she said in a drowsy state.

"I couldn't sleep so I played Backgammon on the computer."

"Oh… right… night…"

And with that she'd slipped back to sleep.

Sadly, I did not get to sleep straight away despite my joints screaming for rest and my eyelids feeling scratchy. It wasn't always like this between Bella and me. When we first married, we would lay in bed looking at each other and smiling into each other's eyes. I would have said something like 'I love you' and she would reply 'I love you, too'. Then for more emphasis, I would say 'no, what I mean is, I really love you'. Love making was simple and uncomplicated. I would climb on top of her gently, my weight on my forearms and slip easily into her. Moving in and out of her was so natural and when I came inside her it was not without advance notice as I was always a bit noisy as my orgasm tore through me. She often said, 'don't wake the neighbours!' I said that if the neighbours were to make any comments about the noise, Bella could always tell them I suffered from cramp.

It should have been obvious to me at that time, but sex seemed to be more for my benefit than hers, or rather, both of us. She rarely appeared to get as much satisfaction as I did, and she was certainly not as adventurous.

I remember being in a friend's swimming pool together one warm summer evening. The light was fading, and we were the only two left. I swam up to her as she was standing beside the wall and put my hand between her legs and pulled her swimming costume to one side. I had already released my erection and managed to enter her in one clever co-ordinated movement. I guess I was hoping she might have relished the spontaneity and amorous approach I had taken. Actually, she stiffened and squirmed to get away from me. I stayed inside her and made some joke that if I pulled out now, she might sink.

Despite the mild rejections, it didn't stop me from trying to make love to her. In our younger days I think we were still quite naive and wrapped up in the euphoria of young sweethearts recently married and with no children. I was twenty-four when we married and Bella was not yet twenty. Were we too young to know any better?

***

It was now early March and the unrest in me was growing steadily. I had been told by several friends that if your home life or your work environment is good, then you can get by comfortably enough; however, if both are bad you run the real risk of mental breakdown. I realised this could be happening to me. I started to do reckless things, well reckless by my nature. I was determined to get the motor bike back on the road. Jerry's widow, Anya, had already offered me Jerry's old Honda bike which was older than my Kawasaki and probably just as powerful. I fantasised about tearing through the Lincolnshire countryside on either bike at some breakneck speed to cure the rage that had built up.

***

John came by one evening with some drawings he had been sent from an architect who needed several steel beams designed for a renovation project. It was always good to see John and I persuaded him to go to the pub for a quick one. I told him about the episode with Bella pushing me away. It had happened more and more often recently, and I had no inkling why she was acting like this. There were occasions when I asked her and all I got was 'nothing' or 'I don't want to talk about it'.

'It' was the thing I needed to know. As an engineer, if I know 'It' then I could try and find a solution to 'It' but all I got was nothingness.

I realised John was going through his own demons as his relationship with Maria had not been good since the motel episode. He and Maria had tried marriage counselling with some degree of success, but I couldn't imagine Bella ever agreeing to go with me.

I confessed to John that one night when Bella had flatly refused to talk about our issues and refused to be intimate, I rather clumsily pirouetted on the bedroom floor naked with an enormous erection and asked her if she could see an on/off switch, because I fucking well couldn't!

John thought that was both crass and funny in equal measure.

"Look," he said. He often started sentences with the word, look. "Maria and I are trying a new technique called Masters and Johnson, you could try that."

"Does it work?"

"Not really," he said, "not for me, but I agreed to give it a go."

I was always suspicious of these new sexual 'breakthroughs', especially coming from America that claim to resolve marital problems. I started to suspect Bella was having an affair but then dismissed that because she was never really into sex in the first place. In my naivety I thought she would mellow and come to enjoy it eventually, if anything the opposite was happening.

"Look, why don't the two of you go away for a few days and see if that helps."

"I'm not sure if more of me will make it even worse," I said resignedly.

"You always seemed good together whenever I see the pair of you."

"Bella is very good at putting on a show for public consumption. No one really knows what goes on behind closed doors do they?"

"Very true," he said, and that was the end of the conversation as he was keen to move on to discuss when I could get the calculations for the beams done. I suggested next Sunday and that was fine, he'd pick them up in the morning.

"Not too early, you never know, I may get lucky."

We grinned and looked at each other knowing that it wasn't going to happen.

***

The next day, I had a bizarre phone call from an old student's mother.

"Mr Avery, it's Jane Randall, Matthew will not be in today as he has a cold or flu."

"Sorry to hear that Mrs Randall, but why are you telling me?"

"Well, you're his course tutor aren't you?"

"Well, I was but we haven't seen him since October. We believed he had dropped out and found an alternative subject at another school or college, or rather that was what he told his mates here."

There was a period of tense silence for a moment and then she said, "but, he's been coming to college every day."

"Pardon?"

"He's caught the college bus from Stamford every day."

Before she hung up, she promised to investigate it further and let me know what was happening.

During the afternoon I received a call from Mr Randall. Apparently, young Matthew was indeed getting the bus everyday into college but then jumping onto the shuttle bus into the city of Lincoln and spent the day in amusement arcades, cinemas, coffee shops or anywhere else he could hang around before reversing his travels home again. I thought my life was difficult and I didn't want to be in that boy's shoes that night.

***

I cannot remember how it happened, but a local charity contacted me indirectly about a practical project that my students could participate in. The charity was looking for someone to set out a car park and access road, with associated drainage for rainwater gullies, etc., and wondered if we could do that. Why not? It would be something tangible and real for the lads. They were certainly up for it when I suggested it to them.

"Do we get paid?" said Dan.

"Are there girls working there?" said Tom.

I said, "If we do this, you will need to be professional and represent the college with good intent. It will be a good learning exercise for you."

I was cross with myself for saying that they should represent the college in this way after all that I had gone through. The college can get screwed as far as I was really concerned. Another indicator, if one was needed, that I had got close to the end. The actual day itself was fun but bloody hard work supervising twenty-four students (actually it was twenty-two as two of them cried off with illness). It was great to watch little teams setting up levels on the tripods, theodolites set over corner points and swinging right angles, erecting profile boards using sledgehammers and cross boards for drainage runs, marking out inspection chambers with yellow spray paint and pulling fifty metre tapes across the site to check diagonals. Although it was a hot day, they wore their fluorescent waistcoats and hard helmets without complaints. I took a moment to survey my own surveyors and became quite emotional. I wanted to hug each of them, but I know what Ben would say.

I remembered a moment back in the classroom a few weeks earlier when two or three of them were scathing of homosexuals. It was not atypical of them to talk like that, and I rebuked them by saying they should be more tolerant in today's society.

'Anyway,' I said, 'statistically about one in fifteen are gay now. You have done enough mathematics to know that means that there is a strong possibility that at least one of you is gay'. They looked around furtively at each other with new interest, but I persisted. 'As a matter of fact, I know there is one person who is gay here. If you give me a kiss, I'll tell you who it is.'

I found humour was always the best way to ease tensions.

The charity was great afterwards. The lads were royally treated to tea, sandwiches and cakes but most preferred Coke, chocolate and ice cream. And yes, there were girls there although Tom was quite shy around them.

Chapter 3

I must have missed the advert in the TES, but John phoned me one evening to say that they were looking to appoint a Senior Lecturer in Structural Design at Manchester University from next September. He had seen the advert in the 'New Civil Engineer' magazine. I had stopped my subscription to the ICE a few years earlier as I had become disillusioned with the Institute. They appeared to have become self-serving and arrogant with their stringent demands to become Chartered. It felt like those at the top had been pulling up the ladder behind them. John had become Chartered, but it had taken seven years in total to get there and in retrospect he thought he might not have bothered had he realised the slog and demands that would be put upon him. Architects on the other hand become Chartered when they graduate, a much better system.

The next day I was actually quite excited to get to college to see if the advert was in the TES. It wasn't. A quick search on the ICE's website though did locate it and I poured over the qualifications required to apply. I even searched Manchester University's website to see the same advert just to confirm.

Honours degree or post graduate studies in Civil or Structural Engineering. Check.

Proven track record of structural design in standard materials. Check.

At least three years teaching experience. Check.

Two professional references. I'd make sure that was bloody check too.

I had time to phone the HR department at Manchester and secured the application form to be posted to me before I went to teach at nine a.m. I quite enjoyed teaching the Critical Path Analysis and subsequent Gant diagrams that morning and the students were into it too. Normally, I hated planning for critical paths as I found them tedious and uninspiring. That was not to say, I didn't value them, but my passion was for design subjects.

***

The euphoria and excitement were like a guilty pleasure for me during the whole of that day. Nothing was going to go wrong today. It was during the cycle ride home when realisation kicked. What was I going to say to Bella?

"Look, Donna," I implored, "Nothing will probably come from it, but it will be a good experience to try for an interview."

"Well why go for a job when you have no intention of doing it?" was her reasoned reply.

I hadn't said that I didn't want it but equally I hadn't said that I did either.

"There's lots of advantages for trying." I continued.

"What exactly? It's more unrest and distraction." Her legal work serves her well.

"It will show the college that I am not to be pushed around and will give me an opportunity to see what's out there, gain experience and give me an edge". I realised that the last two statements were rubbish, but I was running out of ideas and resolve.

"Well, you know my feelings but if that is really what you want then it's up to you." Wow, did she really say that? Then the *coup de grace*. "What are you going to say to the boys about moving away, leaving their schools and pals, our parents, our friends, this house and I will have to leave my job too. Is that what you want?"

I did agree it was a lot of upheaval and totally unnecessary.

I still filled in the form though.

***

John was very happy to write a reference for me, after all we had worked in the design office for about three years and he knew what I was capable of when it came to structures. That one was in the bag. I was pleasantly surprised to see how effusive he was in his character assessment of me and my abilities. I just wish Maria was more aware of how wonderful John is. He needs the love and support of a good woman, and it may not be her, sadly. I wonder if John thought the same about me and Bella. He is too good a friend to challenge him in that way and get him to express an opinion, whatever he may secretly think.

The second reference (technically it should be the first, but what the hell) would need to come from my Head of Department, Kevin Shields. He was slimy and had somehow negotiated his way up the greasy pole from teaching brickwork originally. It was always the way wasn't it, that someone who is totally incompetent is pushed upstairs to get rid of them. Kevin was just the epitome of that. He didn't like me and that was mutual. I had no respect for someone who didn't make decisions, delegated everything, laughed too much to cover his incompetence and was never available to meet any of his staff. He could have done a lot more to protect me from the injustices during the 'Jack Daniels' episode but chose not to do so and hung me out to dry (sorry, that's not a good phrase under the circumstances, but you get my drift). He was often not in his office as he was on the golf course a lot of the time anyway. Someone jokingly said that he had his name written on the bottom of his shoes in case he was so far up the arse of the managers that we knew who it was.

This should be a piece of cake.

"I would like you to write a reference for me, Kevin." I was surprised at my own self confidence. "I am applying for a university post in Manchester."

"Really? Well, we would be sorry to see you go, Phil. When will this position start?"

"Next academic year, I guess. September the first?"

He was clearly unimpressed as he played down my ambition. "I think you are making a big mistake as universities are not going to be interested in recruiting from the FE sector. There must be a vast pool of researchers, readers and better qualified candidates to fill the vacancy." Had he spoken to Bella?

It was time to play my only trump card. "Well, I could forget it and stay here to continue our close association and working practices for many years to come." I smiled, trying to avoid it becoming a grin.

The game was up, and he knew it. By the next afternoon, I had a glowing endorsement from him wishing me every success for the future. What a slime ball.

**

The interview was to be held during the Easter break fortunately. I received a letter confirming the details for the day and I read and re-read it to make sure I hadn't missed anything. I found my degree certificate from Bristol and felt slightly embarrassed that it was only a second class honours and I hoped that they would not judge me too harshly about that. It was going to be a three-hour journey across the Pennines and the road is not great. I needed to be there by 10:00 a.m. for registration and to meet the other candidates.

It was a Thursday morning, and I was up at five a.m. Showered, dressed, I collected everything I needed and set off at six a.m. I was giving myself an extra hour as I wanted to be there on time. Driving across the Pennines with the sun streaming behind me and illuminating the countryside in front of me beckoning me on, was both uplifting and empowering.

I reached the designated car park at eighty-forty-five a.m. and felt foolish at my early arrival but decided a quick walk around the place may be sensible, however, I sat in the car instead and tried to compose myself. I phoned Bella to say that I had arrived safely but had to leave a message as she was on her way from the child minders to her office.

"Good morning, Phil Avery," I said opening my hand to be greeted by Simon Ostler who was the Materials Lecturer and would be sitting on the interview panel. He seemed very pleasant, but then, isn't everyone in this scenario?

I was the first to arrive, so having negotiated the workings of the tricky coffee dispenser on the table in the reception area, I sat by the window facing the door to observe others coming in. There were going to be four of us apparently and I tried not to be overawed by the calibre of the others in the room as they arrived one by one. Next to arrive was a young black man who looked Nigerian perhaps (it turned out he was from Uganda), but he spoke so quietly that I wondered how he would cope lecturing a hundred plus students in a lecture hall. The third candidate was a very smartly dressed man approaching his sixties, or beyond, who had been in industry all his life and was hoping to finish his career in academia. The final candidate arriving in a sweat at nine fifty-five a.m. was an Eastern

European whose strong accent made him difficult to understand.

For the past hour, I had oscillated between walking out there and then, getting into the car and driving back to beg for forgiveness from Bella and promise never to do anything so rash again and then the other side of me saying, 'you can do this, Phil'.

With the other candidates in the room, I took a deep breath. I stood a chance here, I thought.

We toured the facilities; the materials testing labs where Simon could wax lyrically about their non-destructive testing programme for prestressed and post tensioned concrete. I met the technicians and the computer guys, the fluids lab where there was research going on into earthquake foundation design, the transport labs testing frictional resistances for the tyre industry. It reminded me so much of my undergraduate days in Bristol and the newness of it then was rekindled once more.

My interview was first, well it would be with a name like Avery, and at noon precisely I was wheeled into the darkened room with six nebulous faces behind the expansive desk. I was introduced to everyone but who remembers all those names? I did remember Professor Johnson-Peters chairing it, as all I could think of was why double-barrel such two common surnames? I managed to unscramble my brain sufficiently well to give some sort of coherence to my replies regarding the design of reinforced concrete, steel and timber.

One curved ball that came my way was, "You don't appear to have done much research work?"

My reply was something along the lines that I had been in a catch twenty-two situation and was never in a position to do much. I also rebutted it by saying what did they want? Someone with proven research or an effective teacher? I added that I would like to do some research though.

"Such as?" Came another voice.

I had always been interested in structural defects and would like to do more at looking at chemical erosion of reinforced concrete and the effect of spalling (the degradation of concrete around steel reinforcing bars). I don't remember other individual questions, but I was asked to give a strength and a weakness of my teaching style.

I wasn't expecting that one, but my answer was, 'my strength, I think, is my empathy with students and the trust we build together; however, that could also be my weakness as the students could become over familiar'. Well, I thought that was an accurate assessment and it was well received.

For those who are not in education may be surprised to hear that the candidates must decide on the day if they will accept the post if it was offered to them. Such was the nature of the beast that all four of us were sitting in an anteroom at three p.m. following a further tour with Simon of the teaching facilities and lecture theatres. I was thinking Simon had had a long day.

It seemed interminably long but at three forty p.m. Simon came out and said, "Mr Avery, could you re-join us?" The position is mine then.

Professor Johnson-Peters smiled, stood up, shook my hand and formally offered the post with a starting salary some eight thousand pounds greater than my current one with a six thousand pounds re-location package. Wow, I was rather taken aback.

"Thank you all very much. Is it possible for me to think about this?" I said in a very concerned way.

"It's not the normal practice," Prof J-P said, and he looked around at his fellow interrogators. He went on. "Why do you need more time?"

"It's just a big move for me, I would love the opportunity to come here but there are considerations on the home front." I needed to be honest here, I was on a precipice.

Prof J-P had a warm kindly face, and he did not disappoint. "Well, we are not going to appoint any of the other candidates. How long do you need? Can we expect an answer by Monday?"

"Absolutely. Thank you," I said with as much warmth and gratitude I could muster.

**

The journey home was a mixture of excitement and dread. Excited at the prospect of lecturing to undergraduates in the field of engineering I love and dread at the forthcoming conversation with Bella.

It was seven p.m. when I arrived back home and it had been a long day.

Bella said, "If you're quick you can catch Sebastian before he goes to sleep, he's had his bath."

I went quickly up the stairs. "Sebastian?" I whispered as I pushed open his door.

"Dad!" He flung his arms around my neck as I sat on the edge of his bed. "Can you read me a story?"

"Barn on Fire?"

"Yes, and 'Pig Gets Stuck' too." He knows exactly how to manipulate me and abuse my empathy I thought.

***

The weekend was full of 'what ifs' and 'what nots'. I had used up my supply of mental agility and dexterity on Thursday in the interview as well as negotiating the treacherous A57 there and back but this was going to be an even bigger challenge.

Q "If you take it, when will you start?"

A "1st September."

Q "Will we need to move before that?"

A "No, we couldn't sell quickly enough anyway."

Q "Do we need to take the boys out of school in September?"

A "No, not until we are settled in Manchester."

Q "Where in Manchester? Alice says it's a dump."

A   "We can find an area we like and a nice house."

Q   "So what will happen after you start, and we are still here?"

A   "I could rent a flat, it's too far to travel every day."

Q   "How can we afford two properties?"

A   "Well the re-location package can offset the cost."

Q   "What of my dad? His sciatica is getting worse, and mum can't always cope."

A   "We can find a way to cope, nothing is off the table."

Q   "What about the Choral Society? I love that."

A   "I know, Donna, but there is other choral groups, I'm sure."

The first round of enquiry was over when she said, "Will you stop calling me Donna!"

***

I met John for a drink at 'The King's Head' briefly on the Saturday evening. He was genuinely pleased for me.

"You'll take it then?"

"I think so," was my cagey response.

"Look, you are not happy at the college, you love structural design, you have great rapport with students, your dress sense is shit and you have no sense of humour." His grin was followed by, "you'll fit in there perfectly."

Despite everything, all the chains and ropes tying me down, I could now feel them snapping one by one.

As it was the Easter holidays, I had a real and meaningful time with the boys. Bella was at work and would be home at one p.m. as usual. I let the boys watch 'Toy Story' again, despite the fact that the weather was good, and they should have been outside enjoying the sunshine. We could do something together later. Besides, I needed time to compose myself and phone the University's Engineering Department. I had the direct number for the Faculty Secretary. I stood in my office upstairs. I always think that important phone calls like this are best made standing rather than sitting.

"Engineering,", was the reply.

"Oh, good morning, it's Phil Avery here. I promised to phone Professor Johnson-Peters this morning."

"Hold the line, Mr Avery."

Big breath.

"Hello, Phil," was the kindly voice I had come to respect in just a few days. "Have you and your wife come to a decision?"

"Yes, I would be delighted to accept the offer and thank you for your kindness in all of this."

"Splendid!" he said with genuine warmth. "As I said last week, we were not going to appoint any of the others so we could cut you some slack on this occasion."

"Thank you, Professor." I stopped there because adding Johnson-Peters seemed excessive.

"Not a problem, dear boy, I will get Mrs Ahmed to send you all the necessary documentation and we will welcome you in the new academic year. If you need more information about syllabus content and anything else, talk to Simon Ostler in the first instance. I will ask Simon to act as your mentor for the first year."

"Thank you again. I am really looking forward to it."

"Bye, Phil, have a good summer."

I certainly intended to do so. I'll paint that bloody fence with preservative now.

* * *

The conversations with Bella were strained for the next few days while she mulled over the prospect of her life being turned upside down. She agreed that as I was the major breadwinner and a move to Manchester was sensible, the boys could find good schools, possibly better than those in our rural idyll and houses were cheaper in Manchester.

I had been sowing these seeds in her mind for a while, but I was not sure they would germinate.

The choral group met the next Friday, and we were planning our next production, Mozart's 'Requiem' as a summer performance. I really liked the Requiem as it was so deep and poignant, and we were also meeting up with the orchestra a couple of weeks afterwards for a full rehearsal. It was during a break in practices that Bella dropped the bombshell that we may be leaving the group after this performance. It seemed a bit premature to announce this as we were not going to move for several months yet, possibly not until the New Year or even longer.

I think it was her way of getting sympathy and support from our friends against the common foe; me!

"Oh, Bella, we are sorry to hear that."

"Really? You will be greatly missed by us."

"But you've been the mainstay of our group."

I had to explain to the bemused company, as humbly as possible, what was likely to happen for the two of us and as a family. I thought it a little unfair that Bella dropped that little grenade without talking with me first but then had I not done something similar?

Several members of the group were quite pragmatic, pointing out that the group was always transient, people move in or move away. I was starting to find allies all over the place.

Graham reminded us that David and Anna had moved to Manchester last year. That was true, David had secured a research post at the University Hospital specialising in stem cell research or something similar. Perhaps we could drop in on them and they could give us a few pointers about the city, places to go, and more importantly, places to avoid.

Bella raised her eyebrows but did not dismiss the idea.

***

At home, things had not improved much between us, but we were good with the boys. Francis had his thirteenth birthday just three days after Sebastian turned six. That was good as birthday celebrations could take place together much to the annoyance of both of them. Francis's friends were too rough, and Sebastian's friends were scared of the bigger boys. We compromised by me taking the bigger boys to McDonald's and paintballing and Bella had a typical tea party at home for Sebastian's little friends. A couple of the other fathers helped me ferry the boys to the paint balling and onto McDonald's and it was good to get other perspective views on our imminent move across the Pennines. One of the dads originated from Bolton and he was complimentary about the beauty of the moors and the stunning landscapes.

"You'll love it there," he said. "After all, it's a bit flat and featureless here."

I don't know why, but I felt rather annoyed and wanted to defend the reputation of my birthplace. I quickly told myself to forget it. In the end all these little snippets of information were actually making the prospect of the move more attractive.

***

That night was probably one of the low points in our relationship. No, it was the lowest point to date. I know I should have taken into consideration that she had spent the last couple of days arranging Sebastian's tea party and games. The actual day itself was fraught entertaining a dozen hyper six-year-olds, even with her mum and a couple of other friends helping, but I was starting to buzz again.

It wasn't late, eleven p.m. or so when we slipped into bed. I pushed the duvet back and started caressing her feet and licking along her shins. Childishly, I thought it better to start here as there were teeth at the other end! I ignored the stiffening of her body and the perceived but silent 'tut', but I was a man on a mission. Her thighs came into view and my excitement grew as I was moving closer towards her, well to be polite, her vulva, although there were a host of other words I may have used. I didn't even get to base one.

"Oh, for God's sake!" she said in a quiet shout designed to deter me but not wake the boys. "You are not serious?" It was rhetorical and no answer was actually expected or needed. She continued to highlight why my advances were wholly inappropriate. "I have been up since seven preparing food for this bloody party, cooked meals for us, cleaned the house, moved the furniture around, put up decorations, sorted out party bags, cleaned up sick from the carpet..." 'Too much jelly and ice cream,' I thought. "...and now this!" she said with real emphasis.

"I just thought..." I started in my defence but was quickly interrupted.

"Yes, we know what you thought. It's all about you, isn't it?"

"Donna..." I said softly, "what's really the matter?" That triggered it, I had lit the blue touch paper.

"Don't 'Donna' me! You're always the same, I'm supposed to be the submissive wife whenever you want to fuck and be grateful for it." As if that wasn't hard enough to bear, the final parting shot made me see red. "Why don't you go into the bathroom and have a wank?"

We didn't have a spare room, apart from the box room converted to my study, and that was too small for me to kip in. I didn't want to watch porn again as it never really satisfied the intimacy I needed. I certainly wasn't going to relieve myself in the bathroom! I was off like a scolded cat. Quickly pulling on some jogging pants and T-shirt I went downstairs and picked up the car keys and was off into the night. It didn't really matter where I was going as I certainly hadn't expected this. I have no idea where I ended up, but it was somewhere near the coastline by The Wash. I turned the engine off, grabbed the travel rug and got out and sat on a grassy dune on the marshland and allowed the fresh air to wrap me in its comforting arms. The calls of the Lapwings, Curlews, Turnstones, along with other accompanied soloists, was for a time, better than any symphony or choral work. I started to well up, something I hadn't done since Jerry's death.

In my haste to get out of the house I'd forgotten my phone, house keys and wallet. Once the red mist had subsided, I needed to think about what happens next. Options were severely limited, and I would need to go home for the boy's sake if nothing else. I let the serenade continue for another hour until the sun started to colour the dawn in front of me. For that brief moment, the sun was rising just to greet me, the birds were singing just for me, the cool breeze was holding me close and lovingly. I really did cry then.

I wasn't sure what to do when I arrived back at six a.m. Was Bella asleep? How do I get in without disturbing the family? My anxiety was short lived as I had just got out of the car when the front door opened. Bella stood there in her dressing gown and she looked like she hadn't slept either.

"Why did you do that?" she said softly. "Didn't you realise I would be sick with worry?"

I did the only thing I could. I held her in my arms, said sorry with genuine concern and kissed her forehead. We made a cup of coffee in silence and eventually fell into bed about half six.

Her hand went to my groin, and I pushed her away and said, "It's OK, I'm fine, really, I am." I didn't tell her, obviously, but I had deposited my seed in the sand dunes.

Chapter 4

Monday came and we were still on holiday from the college. Bella had gone to work as usual; the weather was miserable and so I felt justified in letting the boys watch 'Finding Nemo'. I had two important letters to write that day, my resignation letter to the college (which I was looking forward to writing) and my acceptance for the post at Manchester (which I was very much looking forward to writing).

A resignation letter is a work of beauty for me as I could summarise. 'Fuck off you bastards' in a very polite and courteous manner. You can include phrases like 'it has been a pleasure to work with such esteemed colleagues' which translates to 'I can't stand the sight of them' and 'the past seven years has been rewarding and fulfilling' can be translated to 'what a waste of bloody time'. My cynicism started to bug me, as I am not really like that and I will miss some of my colleagues and I will definitely miss the students. Having the opportunity to shape the future careers of 'school children' coming in naive and ignorant of the real world of commerce and industry into young professionals destined for, well, anything. My hope is that these lads (and they were all lads, sadly) will become surveyors, architects, engineers, contracts managers of the future. Will they remember Mr Avery? possibly not, but it didn't matter. Mr Avery will remember them.

An acceptance letter too can be a thing of beauty. 'I am looking forward to the challenge of this exciting opportunity within the university' means exactly that. I was looking forward to it. I really couldn't believe my luck. I was excited by the prospect of having one hundred and twenty undergraduates in a lecture theatre showing them how to design steel beams, concrete slabs, masonry piers, timber posts, etc. I had contemplated writing a textbook about the subject, after all, there were books on individual materials but not, as far as I could see, a tome which covers them all. I stopped myself from daydreaming too much, I wasn't even there yet.

***

The telephone seemed to ring for some time before it was answered by a man's voice.

"Hello, David Golding."

"Hello, David, this is Phil Avery, do you remember Bella and I from Lincoln Choral Society?"

"Oh, yes, of course. Bella with the clear descant and you with your own obscure version of tenor singing." His humour clearly hadn't waned.

"Er, yes," I wasn't expecting that response. "Well, the reason for ringing you, apart from taking abuse, is to let you know we too are moving to Manchester."

"Excellent," he said. "We'll have to meet up sometime."

This prompted a useful conversation that lasted a good forty-five minutes of us swapping information about his work, my new post, Anna's work as a freelance journalist, Bella's possible future job in law, schools in the area, nice areas to live, choirs, etc. I never had the opportunity to talk to Anna as she was out of the house at the time, but Bella got onto the phone to have a few words with David. This all culminated in an arrangement that we could pop in and see them during the summer, and they will show us around. It couldn't have been better.

***

"Tell us a joke, Sir."

"Look, we've only got twenty minutes left, and I want you to find those areas under the graph curves." We were using applications of integration. "Has anyone finished question 4?" No one had.

"Oh, come on, sir."

"Right then, what is the integral of one divided by 'book'?" That will challenge them.

"Is that supposed to be a joke?" asked Dan. Dan was so much different since the 'Jack Daniel's' incident.

After a few puzzled moments I told them it was 'logbook'. Some more puzzlement and it needed a trip to the whiteboard to show them that an integral of a reciprocal is log of the denominator.

"You're not very funny, Mr Avery," was the general view.

The news of my impending departure hadn't surfaced yet and I wasn't sure if I should tell them or wait until it was official. They had assessments coming up in a few weeks and I thought they should know sooner rather than later. Besides, I was their tutor and it should come from me directly.

"Look, lads, I have some news for you." They always seemed to know when something serious was afoot and they stopped making asides. "At the end of term, I am leaving the college. I have a new post at Manchester University, starting in September."

"Please say that was a joke, sir?" said Ben, accepting the fact that it wasn't a joke.

I was surprised at the effect it had on them and they were generally subdued. We finished the last fifteen minutes of the lesson talking about my new job, what will be happening next year, their options, the new staff joining the department to replace me and others, including Jerry Unwin's replacement. This had been my first teaching post and I surprised myself how traumatic it was for me, let alone them, to the reaction of this impending separation. Trust and admiration has to go both ways and they had shown me that, and I, in turn, had tried to do the same for them. I wondered if I had done the right thing when I looked at them. I knew deep down I had but it didn't make it any easier.

A few days later I arrived home earlier than normal as we had a meeting with Relate, the Marriage Guidance Counselling service. I was intrigued by the name Relate as it did seem more upbeat than Marriage Guidance. I was surprised that Bella had agreed to go because of her reluctance when I first suggested it several months earlier. The babysitter duly arrived by five-thirty but we did not say where we were going, and she had our phone numbers in case of emergency.

Upon arrival we were shown into a brightly coloured room with three armchairs discretely positioned; a coffee table adorned with a neat box of tissues. Venetian blinds across the window, flower vases on the shelf and a filing cabinet in the corner. If I had to describe what I anticipated the room to be like before I went in, I couldn't have done it any better.

Our counsellor who was in the room with us (Bella had insisted upon a woman) was a grey-haired retired lady, warm, genteel and caring but I wondered how deep this veneer went. After introductions, we were asked to say why we thought we were there and how we thought this session might help us.

"Who would like to go first?" said the kindly voice.

Bella did not want to start, and as I had arranged this meeting, I felt duty bound to get the ball rolling. I talked about how we were good with the kids, but sexually we seemed to be distancing ourselves. I may have unkindly said that I felt like a male spider approaching a mate not knowing whether I'd be lucky or get eaten alive. That did not go down well with Bella nor the kindly face. I stopped short of giving details about any episodes for the purposes of discretion and to save our (or rather, my) embarrassment. After five minutes I dried up and it was Bella's turn.

She described the massive pressure she felt to perform sexually with me. She was in her words, expected to have sex swinging from a chandelier at any time of night or day. She felt that I did not respect her feelings and was taking her for granted. Bella continued for at least thirty minutes describing my inertia to do things around the house. Not taking more responsibility for Sebastian and Francis. How I had unilaterally decided to take on a new job on the other side of the country with little thought of the consequences.

All this time the kindly face was smiling sympathetically, taking notes and nodding gently along reinforcing the view that I must indeed be some sort of monster and sex maniac. I thought, hang on, we don't have a chandelier.

While all this was going on, I was thinking of the joke about the wife moaning about how her husband ravaged her when she bent down to get something out of the freezer. She was telling her friend how he pulled up her skirt, took down her knickers and pushed into her. 'Oh, said her friend, I wish my husband would do that.' 'Yes, came the reply, but not in the middle of the bloody freezer section at Tesco's'!

I couldn't tell that one to the lads. Could I?

The kindly face stopped making notes and as our session was rapidly drawing to a close, she suggested some things we might try. Firstly, find an evening when we could be alone together for a candlelit dinner of something we both liked with a glass of wine that we enjoy and talk about our day. Secondly, agree a time and place, once a week perhaps, when we could make love; include low lighting, perfumed candles and some gentle music in the background.

I was having serious trouble trying to 'Relate' to the kindly face. Was she in the real world?

Back in the car, Bella asked me what I thought about the session. I lied, of course.

"Well, there's some really good ideas perhaps."

"I'm not a fan of perfumed candles," she said.

"I'm not keen on wine," I replied.

We both laughed. It would, at least, paper over the cracks for a while. Needless to say, we did not make a second appointment.

***

Back in college, I was teaching Material Science.

"So, Young's Modulus of Elasticity is found by dividing the stress by the strain and it is a measure of the stiffness of a material, not its strength. What's going on, Sam?"

I guessed what Sam had been doing and it was wholly inappropriate. He had accessed a porn site on his phone and stupidly forgot to mute it. The moans and screams emanating from his device were unmistakeable and the sounds filled the classroom. In a panic at trying to switch off the sound he ended up inadvertently increasing the volume to such a pitch the performers may well have been in the room with us.

Of course, this should result in disciplinary action, confiscation of his mobile and a report sent to the grease ball head of department. None of us wanted that and I was now getting to be de-mob happy anyway.

Sam was completely red in the face and was giggling at the others and they were giggling back at him. They were at the moment like naughty schoolboys again, and that was their appeal.

It did give me the opportunity to be more paternal and forget about mechanics for a while. I was still their tutor and that meant guidance in all matters.

"Look lads, true relationships are not based on sex and you need to learn that and learn quickly." I was going to have to tread very carefully now. "Imagine you have a girlfriend you really like and respect, would you really want to see her being treated that way so that anyone could look at her lustfully?" I felt comfortable going on. "What if it was your mother or your sister on that screen?"

"I know someone whose sister…"

"Shut up, Ben!" I interrupted. "It is not appropriate."

I wished Bella could have heard me saying all of this.

"Switch the phone off and put it away, Sam, and think carefully in future."

"Yes, think carefully about muting it," said Ben.

I could kill that boy sometimes.

***

That evening, I took Francis to his first cricket practice. The local village had a lovely little cricket club and were running sessions for under fifteens as well as younger age groups. Francis hadn't shown much interest before, but a school friend suggested it to him, and he wanted to go. To be honest, Francis wasn't that sporty, but he did like football, and I took him to matches on a few occasions at Sincil Bank, where Lincoln City played. It was good for father/son bonding but ninety minutes was a long time for him, often, by the second half he wanted to leave, especially if the weather was cold and wet.

This evening was different, the sun was shining and a gentle breeze blew across the recreation ground. He didn't have 'whites' but was wearing tracksuit bottoms and a white T-shirt so he was fine. I recalled my early experiences of cricket and remember how hard the ball was and how it stung your hands when you tried to catch it. Being hit in the field wasn't pleasant either but I liked bowling. Francis had a go in the nets and he looked comical under a helmet and leg pads about two sizes too big for him. He did hit the ball well enough to suggest he had good hand to eye co-ordination. He was only in the nets for about ten minutes but he loved it and wanted to go again.

As an adult I should know better than try to indoctrinate him. I found myself saying things like 'we could go to Old Trafford to watch Test Matches' or 'go and see Man City or United' if we lived closer. The poor boy had no idea of what my motives were as Bella and I had said nothing to them about an impending move. At that moment I felt like a snake in the grass but I wanted someone on my side, even a sweet thirteen year old who still had that innocence and trust that youth gives so freely to a parent.

***

Isn't it strange how fate conspires so many coincidences? The same day I received the contract, induction details for new staff and other relevant pieces of documentation from Manchester; there was also another letter confirming acceptance of my resignation and thanking me for my contributions to the work of the college. If nothing else, this proves it was the right decision. Right?

My cycle ride allowed me to breathe in the fresh early summer air and my mathematical mind worked out that I only had thirty-two cycle rides into college left to go before the end of term. Probably less because I will need the car to collect all my paraphernalia. It is amazing what you accumulate over a period of seven years working in a college.

I made a point of phoning Manchester's Student Union accommodation office to see if they could provide names and addresses of letting agents where I may be able to find a flat. They were very helpful and by noon I had an email listing no fewer than forty agents.

I also realised we will need a second car as public transport to and around Manchester would probably be hopeless. If I went by train, I would have to leave on Sunday afternoon and make one or two changes to get to Manchester Piccadilly. Then I would need to take a bus or tram to wherever I was staying. Then, of course, I would need to cycle through the Manchester traffic or find a convenient bus route or find a tram route. I had a lot of things to sort out but I liked problems to solve. The biggest knock to my problem solving was knowing that in September, I could be saying goodbye to my wife and two boys on the Sunday and not see them until the Friday night. Life can be hard.

***

"Right, we are doing mechanics," I said. "So, why is a piece of wire like a student?"

Prairie grass was blowing gently across the classroom again.

"Well, they both need a tension to be taut," I said triumphantly, but I still needed to write on the board.

A TENSION TO BE TAUT

and underneath that:

ATTENTION TO BE TAUGHT

Actually, they liked that and several of them copied it in the back of their folder to impress their parents later.

I was pleased to note that apart from the three or four UCAS references I had written earlier in the year, more than half of them had also made applications to Uni and the others were now considering it. There were a few lads who would like to give it a go, but their parents could not afford that sort of luxury and they were encouraging them to find good jobs in and around Lincoln. I could certainly help here as I still had contacts with various professional firms in the area. For example, a ground working firm needed a trainee quantity surveyor in the summer and someone else was looking for an architectural technician. John had mentioned that they could probably employ a couple of lads to act as chain boys for the summer. A chain boy sounds 'slavish', but they are land surveyor's assistants. The students were impressed when I told them about surveying with chains, a chain is actually twenty-two yards long (the same length as a cricket pitch) and was a surveying technique used by the Romans two thousand years ago. They probably said it was 'boring' at the time but I was surprised how many of them actually remembered it.

The following week was assessments.

Each of the eight subjects they had been studying had a mini exam. It only contributed about thirty percent of the overall mark to the final grade as the other seventy percent had been assessed by projects and TCA's (time controlled assignments, bloody acronyms, eh?). Some of the students were still very much borderline as to whether they would pass or not. They may need to do resits or improve the quality of their project work. I had arranged special catch-up sessions in my lunchtime and they could bring sandwiches and drinks into the room, even though it was against the rules, and we could thrash through some of the problem areas. Maths, in particular, was tough for them. It was a hive of activity for the most part and you could only salute those lads 'running' just to 'catch-up'. It was warm and sunny outside, yet they still chose to come and do the additional work.

It was in one of these sessions, I happened to mention that during your lifetime you will only use about one third of your brain capacity.

It was Sean who said, "What happens to the other three quarters?"

I burst out laughing at the nonsense of his response, but the others all looked at me with some suspicion and curiosity. One by one, they started to laugh when they realised the mathematical impossibility of Sean's comment. Eventually, Alex had to explain to Sean that if you minus one third you get two thirds, not three quarters. Sean looked embarrassed but laughed too. He who laughs last, only just got the joke.

***

The last week of term ended more with a whimper than a bang. I wasn't sure what to expect but everything seemed low key and casual. It was like the college year just took a long dying sigh and everything stopped.

My students drifted off without really saying goodbye apart from the more astute who considered this moment as a significant one, pivotal even. James and Ollie in particular made a point of coming to see me and presented me with a homemade card on which they had penned several of my jokes and written in large letters 'Good Luck in Manchester — You've been the Best'.

I wanted to take a photo of the whole group before we all went our new ways but sadly it never happened. It was like trying to herd cats during that last week. Besides, I had quite a lot of administration to complete; final assessed grades, marked exam scripts, proof of curriculum content covered, student portfolios and projects collated for the exam board and moderator's visit during the summer.

On the last day of term, all the staff congregated in the largest of the teaching rooms to say farewell to colleagues leaving that year. In total, seven of us were leaving, or to be more precise, two were resigning and five retiring. The sparkling wine was warm, the sandwiches dry around the edges and crisps/nuts/cheese biscuits rather hastily presented in cardboard bowls. When it came to my turn for them to bid me a farewell, I had to endure a 'glowing' tribute by that slime ball Head of Department, Kevin Shields, and it required a response. I kept it short and did the usual thing of wishing everyone success in the future and made a particular point of thanking the technicians and support staff. If I recall correctly, I made some reference to football and said that after watching non-league football I was about to observe the Premiership. It was of course a euphemism. Reading between the lines what I was actually referring to was the FE sector and comparing it with the university sector of which I was about to join. I didn't mean to sound arrogant but I had clearly come to the end of my time there. Anyway, the two hundred pounds in book tokens would come in very handy. Thank you.

***

I wasn't able to clear my desk before the end of term and so I came back the following week to do so. It was like visiting the Marie Celeste. No member of the teaching staff was present and there was only a skeleton staff of technicians, administrators and ancillary staff. It took a good three or four hours packing up what I wanted to keep and discarding the rest. I did allow myself a wander around the teaching rooms again and as each door opened to an eerie silence, I recalled the happy hours I had spent with different groups of students over the seven years I had been there. I felt genuinely proud of my teaching, and it affirmed the fact that I was born to be a teacher. I had covered subjects such as Engineering Mathematics, Surveying, Mechanics, Environmental Science and Construction Technology. I wondered how many students had been in my classrooms over the past seven years and tried to recreate their voices in my head; the daft questions, finding alternative ways to describe a topic, explaining the intricacies of differentiation, how to set up a theodolite, listening to their stories from home and all that laughter. Fundamentally, despite my heavy heart at leaving I was keen to move on and excited by the future prospects.

As I walked back to the car to leave for the final time, I took a detour to the loos outside the plumbing workshop. I still can't quite understand why I did that.

Chapter 5

Our family holiday that summer was not dissimilar to the one we had last year. Probably because of all the impending upheaval we didn't want to go abroad or anywhere exotic. We were being pragmatic, or safe more likely. It was just a week on the North Norfolk coast near Sheringham. Bella had found a self-catering cottage and we had been there several times before and we enjoyed being there. It was comforting and relaxing which is probably what we needed at this moment in time. I always think the difference between the two counties, Lincolnshire and Norfolk, is either 'dead slow' or 'dead stop' but not sure which way round. Both are sleepy rural idylls, and I was always relaxed in either place. The countryside can be beautiful when the light is right and the skies are so big.

There was plenty for the boys to do. We could take them to the beach, steam train rides on the Poppy Line, crabbing at Wells harbour, playing on the putting green at Beeston Hills, explore the enormous beaches at Holkham or walks along the cliff tops. It was on one of those walks that Bella and I decided to tell the boys about their dad's new job and the probability of the family moving away. I tried to make it all go with a positive spin by saying there is so much to do in Manchester, but you can't fool kids. Surprisingly, it was Sebastian who spotted more flaws in my plan (sorry, that should have been 'our' plan, but it didn't feel as though Bella had embraced it yet). Sebastian was upset at the prospect and wanted to know what would happen to granny and grandpa, his bedroom, his school and all his friends, his hamster and the list went on. Francis was much quieter, but he could see that Sebastian was right and he wasn't pleased either.

We brought the conversation to a close with the promise of a huge Mr Whippy ice cream with a flake! I tried to placate them by saying it was still early days and nothing is decided yet. Unlike Bella, they couldn't tell whether I was lying or not.

***

A couple of days later, I promised the boys that we could have fish and chips by The Beach Hut Café one evening overlooking the sea. It was warm and there was a gentle breeze coming off the North Sea, but we were all happy, despite the gulls trying to carry out aerial raids on Sebastian's chips. Despite this, they yelled in excitement each time another large white predator came swooping in for a chance meal. Without the pressure from work or home, it was a time when we could truly relax. I felt complete at that moment in time as our little family unit was united.

***

We had been in the cottage for a few days and one evening when Bella and I went to bed I made a point of loving her. I wanted to show her that it was important to me that she should feel loved. Although I could sense she was uncomfortable with my approach she did not stop me from stroking her legs and kissing her ankles. I slowly made my way up the inside of her thighs and spent time moving my fingers gently around her mound, deliberately not touching her lips or clitoris for a few moments so I could look at her. I always loved the sight of her vulva. She did not shave (she would find that a strange thing to do) but she was always neat and tidy. The aroma of her was intoxicating and I closed my eyes and lowered my tongue to her and as carefully and lovingly as possible moved in and around her. After a few seconds, she complained that it was tickling her, and she shuffled up the bed to avoid any further contact.

"Put him in me," she said, "if that's what you want."

She turned on her left side and pulled me up the bed to lay behind her. Her right hand reached round and behind to grasp me, and she guided my cock into her. I wanted to kiss her, look into her eyes, take in the sight of her breasts and watch her facial expressions. Once again, it seemed so mechanical but when you are hungry you will accept even a dry biscuit. After two or three minutes my muffled cries announced my arrival.

Afterwards, I asked her if she had enjoyed that.

"It was OK, do we really need a post-mortem?"

As I lay on my back, I asked myself if she had ever orgasmed. To my knowledge, she had never done so; however, if she had, she may not have made me aware of it and she wouldn't have told me if she had. I had to accept that this was the way she was, and I shouldn't question it. It didn't stop me wondering why she was so reluctant to be open with me, her husband of all people.

***

The telephone rang just three times before it was answered.

"Hello, David Golding."

"Hi David, it's Phil Avery, how are you."

"Good thanks, Phil, how are the family?"

The pleasantries went on for a while because Bella insisted on talking to Anna as well. We seemed to have made all four combinations — me and David, Bella and David, Bella and Anna, me and Anna and established we were all well.

I reminded David of the arrangement we had made and wondered if we could pop in and see them. I say 'pop in' but a three-hour journey with the boys going to Manchester and another three hours back was going to be a logistical nightmare.

Anna made it sound so simple for us, we found a date, Sunday the twenty-fifth of July and we were invited to lunch, she asked what the boys liked to eat and were we vegetarians, then after lunch David would give us a tour

around the area in his car while she stayed and looked after the boys with her two daughters. When we get back, they would explain the public transport system, buses and trams, together with the cycle routes of the university. She would give us a light tea before we went home again. We were so grateful and Bella offered to make a desert and bring it with us. Her kind offer was turned down as Anna was more than happy, no, delighted, to be able to see us again and we needed not to fret over carrying a desert for three hours in the boot of the car.

I had difficulty remembering what David looked like, after all we had only met them through singing and often, either he or I may have been absent due to work commitments. Also, they had moved a year or so earlier. Bella did recall that he had dark rimmed specs and greying hair, but I was none the wiser. I did remember Anna clearly though, she had long strawberry blonde hair which she never tied up like the other singers during concerts, she seemed delicate but strong and had a slightly pointed chin, a bit like Felicity Kendall or Jennifer Aniston. I remember she was attractive in an understated way. What I mean by that; is she rarely wore makeup and had genuine care and concern for others. She and David had been singing with the group for five or six years before their move away.

***

One of the ideas that Bella wanted to experiment with following our trip to the kindly face at Relate, was to arrange a time to have sex. It seemed to me to be so mechanical and contrived and did not leave much room for spontaneity or impulse. The idea was that she would have a bath earlier on a Sunday evening so she was relaxed and would not feel under any pressure. I was not that enamoured with the idea, but I was in a powerless state, she held all the cards and had the control. Even then as we lay in the bed I had to wait until she finished reading her book, invariably, she would drift off and I was left to switch off the light and hope she remembered in the morning.

The number of times I lay wide awake at one in the morning sexually frustrated was more than I could bear sometimes. It resulted in secret trips to the computer to watch porn on the internet occasionally. I hated myself, especially after my talk with Sam and his classmates. It felt very hypocritical but yet, necessary.

I had dallied with the idea of visiting massage parlours years earlier, but it seemed seedy, and I knew I would be embarrassed and self-critical of myself afterwards. There was one occasion I did try it after seeing an advert in a local paper. It advertised 'home visits by qualified masseur' which I understood meant 'prostitute'. It was before the boys were born and I was working from home doing some design calculations, Bella was working full time then. I picked up the phone and started to dial the numbers but after three digits put it down again. A few days later I did the same but hung up after five digits had been pressed.

I always thought that Bella would become more responsive to my love making and advances as we grew together. Sadly, the opposite seemed to happen. Her maternal instinct and hormones cut in sufficiently to quell my desire for a few years when we're trying for children. Oral sex (and in my naivety as a young man, I thought that meant 'talking' about sex — it's true I swear) was not to, well put it crudely, not to her taste and she would always stop at that crucial self-affirming moment. It was so frustrating and upsetting. I used to privately call it the 'Finsbury Park' moment as it was the last stop before the end of the line at 'Kings Cross'.

Eventually, I did make that call and shockingly, a man answered.

"Hello."

"Oh, hello, I am ringing about the advert in the Lincoln Echo."

"Hang on." I heard him shout a name away from the receiver. "Yvonne, telephone for you." Followed by, "hang on she's just coming." I thought that was an unfortunate phrase.

She seemed so pleasant on the phone as I garbled and stumbled my way through a very tense conversation where I at least managed to give all the details; address, time of visit and a false story of having a bad back, hence the need for a masseuse.

**

The next day at eleven in the morning, Yvonne dutifully arrived. She was very neat and tidy with a tight knee length skirt, woollen top, leather boots (that was the giveaway) and carrying a rather oversized canvas handbag slung across her shoulder. She passed the entrance to our previous small, terraced house and knocked on our neighbour's door instead. So, perhaps I hadn't given all the right details. Thinking on my feet as quickly as possible, I opened the front door and said to her.

"Sorry, they are not in. They're both at work."

"Oh," she said and looked at her slip of paper. "I was looking for Phil."

Yes, I had used my real name.

"That's me," I could say with confidence.

"Oh," she said again and looked at her slip of paper and the door number again. We were at 17a, and she was standing outside 17.

Once the confusion had been resolved she came in and I was at a complete loss to know what to do next. I offered her a cup of coffee, which she accepted, and she sat opposite me in the armchair. The small talk was rather bizarre as I struggled to find an introduction. We talked about the traffic, the weather, our décor in the house until I ventured the question.

"What services do you offer?" I said rather lamely.

"Well, I can't answer that question directly."

It took me a moment to realise she was suggesting that this could be a trap and I was something to do with the law.

"Do you do extras?"

She didn't answer but smiled at the entanglement I was getting myself in.

"I mean... do you do hand relief?"

"Yes."

"Oral?"

"Yes."

My heart jumped at that as I didn't want intercourse. Somehow, in my mind, that would have been unfaithful to Bella. We agreed on a price (and believe me, no price was too much for me at that moment) and went upstairs. She couldn't have been nicer to me in that heightened state of anticipation. She stripped completely, rubbed my back with talc (I refused oil as I was concerned about what could be left on the sheets) and she asked me to turn over. If her massage was designed to relieve pressure, well it worked, but all that pressure was now centred in just one place. Her hands moved closer now, and I thought I was going to explode; I could hardly breathe. She went down on me so gently and didn't use a condom.

For a few brief moments that was real ecstasy and as I came in her mouth, she continued her loving care as I gripped the bed sheets tightly and gave out a moan like a feral boar. I thought, 'welcome to Kings Cross'.

***

We pulled up outside David and Anna's house just about noon on that Sunday, slightly earlier than planned as I was keen to look around and I had marshalled the troops back at home in a very precise way to avoid potential delays. The A57 seemed fine this time but then of course it was a Sunday and traffic was less busy.

The house itself was a large Victorian terrace which would have looked resplendent in its hey-day but time had ravaged some of the exquisite features. The window frames, the decorative eaves, the chimney stack and even the paving slabs were all looking tired and jaded. There were still features that exhibited it's past glory like the stained glass in the transom over the front door and the ornate doorbell pull. Francis wanted to pull on that, but we used the modern doorbell instead, after all we don't want to damage anything on our first visit.

It was Jasmine who opened the door and her little sister, Imogen, ran along the corridor after her clutching a teddy bear in one hand and stretching the hem of her skirt with the other. Jasmine was roughly about the same age as Sebastian, perhaps a year or two older, Imogen was nearly four. They stood framed in the doorway and said nothing but just looked at us in puzzlement.

"Hello, hello, hello," said Anna as she came along the corridor in pursuit of her two offspring. I thought that was one 'hello' too few as there were actually four of us.

They couldn't have been more pleasant and welcoming. David took us on a tour around the house and garden (as soon as I saw him, of course I remembered him). Sebastian wanted to play with the doll's house that was in Jasmine's room, and she was the perfect host, even in her miniature world. They moved the tiny pieces of furniture from room to room and created their own story, including a bedroom just for dinosaurs. Francis was not so confident, and he didn't want to leave Bella's side for a while, not until David introduced him to a copy of a Cricket Annual and he was then totally engrossed with the pictures of spectacular catches, off drives and fast bowlers' cart-wheeling stumps out of the ground.

All the time David was showing Bella and I around the place, Anna was preparing everything for lunch. She had refused any help and had planned to put the children in a reception room next to the dining room with a connecting bi-fold door wide open so we were all effectively in one area. Lunch consisted of various salads, dips, quiche, pittas and salmon for the adults. The children had fish fingers, waffles and peas.

I was wrong about David's work, he was actually based at the Royal Infirmary Hospital and involved in clinical research trials. The hospital was about two miles from where they were living off Victoria Park. The university about a mile further on.

Looking at Bella's face as David was driving us around the city after lunch, I could see that she wasn't impressed. I could see that in her mind she was formulating more questions and problems than answers and solutions. I was delighted to see the engineering building hone into view as we approached. It looked different now in as much I was no longer a stranger but will become part of this in a few weeks. I felt a slight warmth at just the sight of the building in which I will be based.

David was saying all the right things as far as I was concerned as he was taking us around. Good schools, nice areas, good choice of houses at reasonable cost, good food outlets, choice of supermarkets, great entertainment, sporting venues and such diverse choirs and music festivals. Of course, I was lapping all this up but didn't let it show. As I was on the rise, I could sense Bella was on the way down, but she didn't let that show either.

Later, when we had returned to the house after the drive around the city, Anna was telling us about potential areas where we could find temporary accommodation and I think we agreed it would not be sensible to move the family at this stage. We needed to take time to find the right house, schools, somewhere for Bella to work. So, in effect I was looking for a single studio flat on a temporary basis and there was certainly a wide choice. Now might be the time to find somewhere before the students return at the end of September.

"You are welcome to come back on your own, Phil, and have a proper look around," said David.

I had been thinking about that as I wanted to explore further the possibility of trains, trams and buses as well. The train journey from Lincoln didn't look much fun as it normally took at least one or two stops including the change at Sheffield.

"Thank you," I said. "I would certainly like to do so."

On the drive back home, I could tell that Bella had retreated to some safe place in her mind and was not keen to get involved in any meaningful discussion about the day's visit. The boys seemed happy enough though and Sebastian, in particular, wanted to go back and play with Jasmine. David had given Francis some other books on cricket and football for the journey home and he was engrossed in them. I knew better than to say anything to Bella at this stage and it may mean waiting for a few days until she surfaced. The journey home had been quiet, apart from Sebastian occasionally talking about what he and Jasmine would do when he sees her again.

Not surprisingly, we did not have sex that Sunday evening.

***

Apart from the odd phone call with my dad, I hadn't seen him properly for some time and I wanted to visit him. Bella suggested I take the boys one morning when she was at work, and I countered by asking her if she wouldn't like to come too.

"No, you go but send him my love."

"He will be sad not see you." I knew I was wasting my time as her mind was set.

It was good to see dad. He was doing fine for someone who had turned seventy-six recently and was keeping busy in the garden of his bungalow in Boston. He had a knack of growing all manner of vegetables; beans, sprouts, peas, soft fruits and yet never plagued by blackfly, slugs or other pests. As a self-employed builder he could turn his hand to most things and I think that influenced me growing up when I started to have a passion for construction, and ultimately, engineering.

I knew exactly what his first question was going to be. "Bella, not with you?"

"No Dad, she is at work." It was accepted as an answer but not as an explanation.

I could see from his reaction that he was disappointed that his only daughter-in-law hadn't visited for some considerable time. He asked if everything was all right between us and of course I lied.

"Couldn't be better." I added, "She is not very happy about the move to Manchester though."

"I am not surprised, are you? She is a Lincolnshire girl, and it will be hard for her."

"I'm a Lincolnshire boy," I said defensively.

"You're different, son, you went to university and seen the bright lights. You want something more and I don't blame you. You've got a good brain and I am pleased for you." I looked quizzically at him, and he said, "I mean it."

It was only a brief visit as it was tricky to entertain two young boys in their granddad's house for long. My mum had died ten years earlier and all the femininity that was once in the house had been slowly eroded and left the inescapable odour, sights and sounds of a widower in residence. That was not to say the house was messy or unkempt, far from it as dad kept the place clean and tidy, it was just, well, different.

***

I was expecting a phone call from John about some steel beams needed for an extension. When the phone rang, I picked it up and instinctively said, "Hello, John."

"Actually, it's David Golding, Phil."

"Sorry, David, I was expecting a call from one of my old design buddies."

"Do you need me to hang up then? I can always ring back later."

"No, no, no it's not a problem. Great to hear from you. Are you and Anna OK?"

"Yes, everything is fine."

David went on to say that he and Anna were talking about our move to Manchester and in short, would I like to lodge with them on a temporary basis until we were settled permanently. There were lots of advantages; I could pay them a nightly rate for just the days I stayed, it would give me, rather us, more time to find the right place to buy, it was close enough to the university that if I wanted to cycle or take a bus, it may be possible, I could babysit for them occasionally, we could go singing together and Anna thought I would be good company for David. David went on to say they had a couple of spare bedrooms, I could have the attic room as it was quiet up there, they had two family bathrooms as well as their own en-suite.

It was such a perfect solution and I think Bella was relieved that I wasn't going to be on my own and we were not going to throw money away on renting a flat full time.

I thanked David profusely and said Bella and I will talk about it and get back to them. After only a few minutes of discussing it, I was able to ring David back and said a very emphatic. "Yes, please. Thank you both so very much."

Chapter 6

Induction day came round a lot quicker than I had anticipated. They were held on the Wednesday, Thursday and Friday before the full term started the following Monday, except students wouldn't be returning in earnest for another two weeks after that.

I arrived at David and Anna's house just after eight p.m. on the Tuesday so that they didn't feel obliged to feed me, I had explained to them beforehand that I wanted to eat with Bella and the boys before I left Lincoln.

It was a warm evening, typical of early September. David and Anna made me feel very welcome and the girls seemed to accept me from the beginning as some sort of surrogate or benign uncle. Not only had Anna provided me with sheets, duvet cover, pillows and towels but also set up a little desk and table lamp for working in the evenings. It was almost like being in my old student flat in Bristol all those years ago, except here it would not be appropriate to put old beer mats on the wall, or posters of 'Yes' and 'Genesis.' The thought had crossed my mind.

I always find sleeping in a new place difficult to start with and that night was no exception. I must have woken two or three times and on each waking the room seemed to take on a differing hue depending upon where the sun was rising.

Anna and I agreed that breakfast would be minimal, and I was happy to have a bowl of cereal or some toast and coffee. She showed me where everything was kept so I could help myself. One thing she was strict about was that I was to put crockery etc., in the dishwasher and not wash things in the sink.

***

The first day's induction was very gentle and started with coffee and biscuits at ten a.m. followed by a presentation at ten-thirty a.m. by, first, the Vice Chancellor, then the Director of Studies and finally the Human Resource Manager. I was surprised how many new members of staff there were, and a quick estimate suggested about a hundred. Later, I discovered it was ninety-four so my estimation was pretty good.

In the afternoon we were directed to each Faculty where we belonged and here the new recruits were just eight in the engineering department and by the time we settled in the civil engineering department, there were just two of us. My fellow newcomer was Frederick Mahler, who specialised in Fluids and Water Resources. Frederick (as he insisted on being called) came originally from Hungary and had a very thick accent. I started to wonder where that other candidate from Eastern Europe ended up after my interview.

"Hi Bella, how are you? How are the boys?"

"We're OK, how is the new place?"

It started to seem so stinted and formal while making these calls to her. I didn't feel comfortable talking on the mobile from within the attic room and even though I would see her tomorrow, as we had now completed the second day of induction, it was almost as though she had become more remote from me than ever within the space of forty-eight hours.

We talked about everything in a mundane and matter of fact way. I really wanted to know what she was wearing, not just her dress but what colour knickers did she have on and which bra. But of course, that was not what she would want to hear, and she certainly wouldn't tell me anyway. What is the saying? 'Absence makes the heart grow fonder'. I started to wonder if it was becoming 'out of sight, out of mind' for her.

***

Turning the key in the door, I was greeted by a flying Sebastian shrieking, "Dad", in a volume designed to startle the neighbourhood. Even Francis made a point of greeting me at the door and a tousle of his hair was sufficient to affirm our bond. The third member of the welcoming committee was sweet as she kissed me gently, but quickly, on the lips and had a smile that said, 'I missed you'. Parting may be sweet sorrow, but in many respects, reunions have a sweet sorrow about them too.

Anyway, the meal that Friday evening was a celebration. It was only pasta and tomato sauce, but we all liked that and there was plenty to chat about. The boys were keen to know more about what I had been doing for the past three days and Sebastian, in particular, asked about Jasmine and the doll's house.

Later, I spoke to my dad on the phone to let him know my news and John rang to ask how it went.

***

John popped in on Saturday morning, not for long as he knew our weekends were going to be special and intense. He brought a set of drawings for a large, detached house with a complicated roof structure and it would need to have steel purlins as well as a cut timber rafter arrangement. John outlined the alignments of hips, valleys and rafters but to be honest, I could have worked that out for myself. Anyway, I promised I would do them during next week in time for him to collect and submit them for building control.

***

If last Tuesday had not been bad enough, Sunday evening was worse. Driving off to Manchester again with Sebastian and Francis framed in the rear-view mirror was gut wrenching but I had to tell myself things would improve.

The next week was not at all stressful as the students were not back and it gave me time to get some teaching resources prepared and to become familiar with the high-tech gadgetry in the lecture theatres. The main theatre could hold three hundred but there was a dividing partition so that two lectures could be held simultaneously to a hundred and fifty students in each. There were six television screens mounted on either the side walls or the ceiling, an audio link with a wireless microphone that you clipped to your shirt, tie or suit jacket, a computerised display table so my notes or anything I needed to refer to could be televised and displayed on the TV screens. There was also an AV control room at the back of the raked lecture theatre for showing slides or film projections. It was really the state-of-the-art facility. I decided that I would try a dummy run and Simon Ostler joined me to show me how the whole system operated. Simon laughed as he recalled that they had spent two hundred and fifty thousand pounds on upgrading the theatre the previous summer and the first time they used the AV room, the technicians, believing they were the only people in the building that day, used a porn film as their test. Simon knew because he was there and had visited the back of the hall when it was in complete darkness, only to be confronted by an image of a couple having intercourse. Simon laughed at the incredulity of spending so much money and the first use was so basic and carnal, but also, typical.

My timetable was issued mid-week and it was encouraging to see that I was not due to start until eleven a.m. on a Monday morning and would finish by lunchtime on Friday. With any luck, I may be able to leave Lincoln on a Monday morning instead of driving on Sunday evening, On Fridays, with some good fortune, I may be able to meet the boys out of school. There are swings and roundabouts of course and I noticed that I had two evening sessions that did not finish until eight p.m. but they were seminars and not main lectures fortunately.

That evening I phoned Bella to tell her about the timetable and how fortunate we were that we may end up having longer weekends but I got the distinct impression she was not that bothered. She may have said something like, 'well there may be other reasons for you to be required on Monday mornings or Friday afternoons.'

***

The evenings with David and Anna were very comfortable and we were all keen to get along as best we could. For my part, I distanced myself in the attic room and had plenty of work to do. Preparing lectures or doing structural calculations to give to John at the weekend. My laptop was essential for both and emailing my calculations to the printer at home was a doddle. In this day and age, it felt that you could work from any place provided you had good internet connections.

***

One Thursday evening, David was late back from work as a clinical trial was at a critical point. I offered to take and collect Jasmine from Brownies; it was only a short walk to the church hall and would free Anna to look after Imogen and prepare dinner.

Anna was in a fortunate position that she could work mostly from home as she was a freelance journalist. Her contracts were sporadic and infrequent at times. She needed to research most of her topics and so spent quite a lot of time in the libraries, public records office and scanning old newsprints collating relevant facts. Having Jasmine in school was convenient, but Imogen was booked into a pre-school this academic year but would join her sister at St Catherine's Primary next year.

"Thank you," she said when I got back from depositing Jasmine at five-thirty p.m. at the hall. "I knew it was a good idea for you to be here."

"It's a pleasure."

"Are you able to collect her at seven?"

"Of course."

"Great, we can eat when you get back. It's only pizza, I'm afraid."

"I love pizza," I said. "Perhaps, I can cook you all a meal sometime."

"Oh no, my kitchen is a mystery known only to me."
It was a clear statement that it was her domain alone.

"OK, I will take you all out occasionally to show my appreciation."

"That would be lovely. The girls feel all grown up in a restaurant."

David didn't arrive home until eleven p.m. but was not concerned about missing dinner, nor it seemed was he bothered about not seeing the girls or having the chance to put them to bed. He just cut a large slice of bread and cheese with a few pickled onions and settled down to watch the news instead.

**

This was going to be a step up. I was used to having groups of young country boys up to twenty in size for construction subjects back at the college. I was about to meet a hundred and twenty second-year degree students and I was the newbie.

The theatre started to fill up with serious looking young men and a few women, pouring in from any of the three entrance doors and sliding along the raked benches to get a good vantage point. All this time I tried to avoid any eye contacts but checked that the camera was working, the TV monitors on, the microphone was secure to my tie via a clip, my papers aligned correctly (for the third time!). It took a good five minutes for them all to congregate and settle by which time my mouth had gone bone dry and I had forgotten what I was going to say as an introduction. I remembered good old Jerry who once met a completely new set of students and said, 'welcome to A level Russian'. At that point there was a slight panic in the students faces and one of them ventured.

"Oh, sorry, sir, we thought this was going to be construction."

Jerry kept a straight face. "Construction?" and then added, "oh, OK, I'll have a go at that then."

I wondered if I could get away with saying, 'Welcome to 16th century English Prose' but I realised that could go horribly wrong and any reputation I may have will be soured forever. I started.

"Welcome to Structural Design 1. My name is Phil Avery, and I will be taking you through this course on the design of all the major structural materials." As if they needed reminding, I confirmed to them. "Timber, steel, reinforced concrete and masonry."

Once I had started, I was fine. I went through the essential reading material including 'Extracts of British Standards for Students of Structural Design' and various other books, for example 'Currie and Sharpe' and 'Trevor Draycott'. It irked me slightly that those authors had 'pinched' my idea of writing a single volume containing all the pertinent design aspects of the materials I was intending to explain over the next few months. Well, that is a book I will not now be producing but I remembered a quote; 'everyone has a book within them, but for the most, that's where it should stay'.

I also started to think about my Bristol days and thought how lucky these students are nowadays. We had to buy all the British Standards ourselves; BS 449 on Steelwork, CP 110 for Concrete, etc.

The hour and a half went very quickly, and I reminded them at the end that I would see them all during the week in their smaller seminar groups to consolidate the material we had covered.

***

"It went really well, Bella." I had started to call her Bella now to avoid annoying her.

"Good," she said, "well done." I could tell her voice was troubled about something.

"What's the matter?"

"Oh, it's Sebastian. He hit my mum today."

"No! What happened?" I was quite shocked as Sebastian loves grandma.

"I don't think he meant it, it was just that mum wanted to come back from the playground and he wanted to stay longer. He just lashed out with his foot and caught her." Bella, sounded quite stressed.

I was pleased that her mum was coming over to the house, at least Bella had company, but I was anxious that this had happened, and it was adding to all our stress levels. I asked if everything was all right now and got the answer that Sebastian had cried a lot but was back to normal.

"Give the boys my love and tell them I am missing them and see you all on Friday." It was all I could do from the end of a phone, but it left me feeling quite useless.

***

A few weeks had passed, and I was really immersing myself in the work. It hadn't taken long to get into some routine, and everything was clicking along nicely. Perhaps it was still the honeymoon period. David and Anna's house had quickly become a second home, but I was keen not to add to the domestic burden and ensured I kept my bathroom clean and tidy, cleaned the floor in my attic room and the stairs weekly (well, almost every week). We had agreed that I would leave them an envelope at the end of each month with the cash to cover the number of nights I had stayed. Jasmine wanted help with her maths and science homework occasionally and when David was still at work, I jumped at the chance to help her. I think the teacher in me was never far from the surface, even when a year three pupil needed help.

The girls never knew what to call me. Often, they didn't refer to me by name at all. 'Phil' seemed over familiar, and 'Mr Avery' was worse. One evening we agreed that I should be called 'Phil' and that was it.

There were some mornings I had time to take Jasmine to school and Imogen to the childminder if my teaching allowed. It did feel strange but also comforting to hold the girls' hands as we walked along the streets together, to the casual observer I was every bit their father, as indeed David was.

It was almost the reciprocal of what was happening at the weekends back in Lincoln.

****

Over breakfast one Saturday morning I broached the subject again.

"Bella, how do you fancy another trip to Manchester to look at houses?"

The answer wasn't 'yes' nor was it 'no'. She started putting up obstacles.

"There is so much going on at the moment to think about that just yet." The list consisted of the boys' schools, her parents' health, her work, the choral group practices, and it's the wrong time of year to be looking.

I realised that this was not a conversation she was prepared for or wanted to engage in.

I also realised that our sex life had virtually stopped as she had given up on having a bath on a Sunday evening and having an early night. Instead, she reminded me that I would have an early start on Monday mornings and so needed a good night's sleep ready for the week ahead.

It was now mid-November, I was wondering if we would ever move to Manchester as a family. Bella had shown no interest in doing so, David and Anna had made it clear they were happy with the arrangement we had, the girls seemed to like me being around, my boys had got use to the situation (aren't kids resilient?) and I was slotting into two roles very comfortably, i.e., a working professional mid-week and a family man at weekends.

I had virtually stopped singing at this point, not just because of the demands of the work but I had lost interest as it was something Bella and I did together. She was still singing with the group in Lincoln and they practised on a Thursday evening. Her mum would stay over to allow her the freedom to get to the sessions. David and Anna had joined a group which sang contemporary songs and I wasn't in to that scene. I still enjoyed church music but hadn't felt an urge to look for anything suitable. I did want to do something else though but couldn't think what. I would wait until my situation settled. One thing I had started doing was swimming in one of the local community pools. I realised I was getting unfit as I was using the car more often than public transport and I hadn't the confidence to cycle in such a big city.

Twice a week I would rise at six-thirty a.m., pull on some jogging bottoms and T-shirt and carry my suit, shirt and tie to the baths. I was often in the water just after seven a.m. when they opened. A quick shower, dress and I was ready for lectures or seminars by nine a.m. I congratulated myself for making the effort and even used the stairs instead of the lifts.

***

It was about this time I had a strange encounter with a girl in the street late at night. I had left college about eight-thirty p.m. and decided to get a kebab or something as Anna knew I wouldn't be back to eat with them. It was convenient that on a few evenings when I was working late, that I would get something during the day on the university campus. On this particular day I hadn't taken that opportunity, so I was driving around randomly looking for a fast-food outlet plus it gave me a chance to become more familiar with another area of Manchester. I parked in a side road but before I could get out of the car, a girl's face appeared at the passenger window. She looked cold and was not dressed for the cool air. Her dark hair clung to the side of her face. She tapped on the window of the passenger door, and foolishly, I wound down the window (why did I do that as David said there are areas that you should be very careful, and I had no idea where I had strayed).

"Are you looking for business?" she said flatly chewing gum at the same time.

"No, I was looking for a kebab." I had noticed there was a kebab shop on the main road around the corner.

It looked as though she thought I was taking the piss out of her. Her face screwed up into a quizzical expression. It obviously needed more explanation.

"Sorry, I am new to this area and was just looking to get something to eat."

She said nothing but just moved down the road into the darker recesses afforded by the inadequate street lights.

Getting out of the car I looked back at her retreat. She was wearing knee length boots and a tight skirt which only just covered her buttocks. It brought back memories of Yvonne all those years ago except this poor girl was trying to make a living on the streets.

I am no great philanthropist, far from it, but to my mind young girls like this are surely in so much danger. I often asked myself why the law couldn't be changed to give these girls a safe place to work, a brothel or massage parlour perhaps. Get them away from preying pimps and with access to better health checks and drug rehabilitation schemes. The answer was obvious really, no government of any colour wants to draw criticism upon itself by dealing with the problem.

After collecting my kebab and eating it in the car, I kept looking to see if she was still around and asking myself where she was now.

***

Christmas and New Year was great. It was a nice time to spend those three weeks holiday back with the boys and Bella. We visited her parents in Scampton on Christmas Day for dinner. They had moved into Lincoln from Louth three or four years earlier for good reasons, they wanted to be closer to their only child and their two grandsons plus their health wasn't great and visits to a clinic were becoming more frequent and necessary. Her dad's sciatica was getting worse, and he was becoming frustrated at his lack of mobility.

Her dad wasn't convinced by my move to Manchester, and he would make a few barbed comments from time to time.

"Do you not worry about leaving Bella on her own all week?" was one such missile. Another was, "you'll regret not being there to see the boys growing up." I was used to these raids but my defence was secure but I never went on any counter attacks. I accepted his concerns and tried to placate him wherever possible.

Boxing Day fell on a Sunday, and we decided to take her parents back to the church at Louth for morning service. It was the place where Bella and I got married eighteen years ago and it all looked so familiar. The choir processed in (there were only eight of them as I guessed several had gone away for Christmas or perhaps, they had done enough singing leading up to the festivities). I turned to Bella and asked her if she would like to still be in the choir? She just smiled and shrugged but it meant that, 'Yes, she would'.

After the service, Bella took her parents to a pub just outside the village for lunch and the boys and I would join them there. We walked along the road to the small bridge and followed a footpath which ran alongside a field and then along a wood before emerging a hundred yards or so from the pub. Along the way I asked Francis if he would like to move to Manchester. He was now in year nine and

I was concerned that if we didn't move before the end of the academic year his GCSE studies may be badly affected.

"I don't know Dad," he said. "I like being here."

"Do you not find it a bit boring though?"

"Not really. I like the school we're in."

He was my son but then again, he was also Bella's son, and he was just like her. I was thinking about my next question when we disturbed two pheasants cowering in the long grass. Francis shrieked with delight and shock as they flew up raucously just feet away. He and Sebastian laughed, and I swear Sebastian did a little jig along the footpath. I decided not to pursue the subject further.

***

"Hi Dad!" I shouted as I pushed open his back door.

"In here, son." He called back.

"Happy New Year, Dad." We were never really tactile, but I wanted to hug him, and he was happy to receive it.

"How have you been son?"

I am glad he asked that question because I wanted to tell him everything. I hadn't seen or spoken to John for a few weeks as there was little private work coming in and there were few opportunities to go down to the pub together. We were going to see my dad as a family together later in the week but I wanted the chance to drive over to Boston to see him on my own.

I started to tell him about Bella's reluctance to move, how the job was going really well, how lucky I was to be able to lodge with David and Anna, about my keep fit programme but fundamentally, and it surprised me to hear it leaving my lips, I am lonely.

"Well, I did say that might happen, didn't I?" said dad all knowingly. He was always very astute and perceptive and that's probably the reason he inspired me.

He opened a couple of bottles of 'Poacher's', and we settled down at the dining table for a heart to heart. His message was simple, find the middle ground where you can survive comfortably, accept your good fortune and don't force the issue with Bella, she will adapt. He reminded me how I loved the job and the opportunities to write papers on structural defects and failures.

I quipped. "Perhaps I can use some of your building projects as examples then."

"Cheeky little sod," was his reply. I felt so much better on the way back from Boston.

Chapter 7

Back in Manchester, I opened the front door after ringing the bell. It always seemed sensible to ring the bell even though I had a key, I didn't want to startle anyone by just walking in unannounced. It was Imogen who ran down the corridor to greet me.

"Hello Uncle Phil," she said. I thought that wasn't the deal but let the epithet pass.

"Happy New Year, munchkin," I said. "Have you had a good time?"

"Yes," and she proceeded to tell me all about her presents.

Jasmine stood smiling and pulling on the sleeve of her cardigan and waited patiently to tell me what she got for Christmas too. After all the details of toy ponies, books, hair slides, games, puzzles (I didn't want to admit I'd given them the puzzles) they led me by the hand, which was quite tricky as I still had my bag over my shoulder.

"Mum, Uncle Phil is here!" Imogen shrieked.

Anna came down from upstairs after sorting out some clothes and laying out some bedding.

"Welcome back," she said. "Did you and Bella have a good time?"

I didn't want to give chapter and verse of everything we had done over the holiday as that would have spoilt the moment. I just said, "Yes, I'll tell you all about it later. How was your holiday?"

"Busy," was her response, "but I'll tell you about it later, too."

Of course, it should have been obvious to me that neither David nor Anna would have too much time to celebrate Christmas as they were not afforded the luxury of three weeks break like me. David was still not back from work, even though it was six p.m., so I settled down on the floor with the two girls and allowed them to show me their presents. Imogen spent a long time telling me all about her Little Pony. All the time, I was wondering what Sebastian and Francis were doing at that precise moment.

Anna was finishing off a sausage casserole with mashed potatoes. It reminded me of the dinners my mum cooked and how warming and comforting that food is on a cold winter's evening.

***

The telephone rang in our staff room and Greg answered it. There were only five of us in that staff room and we were all either structures or materials lecturers and readers.

Greg said to me. "It's for you Phil," and handed me the receiver.

"Hello, Phil Avery here."

The warm and gentle voice of Prof J-P said, "Hello, dear boy, how are things with you?"

"Good, thank you Professor."

"Come and see me this afternoon, Mrs Ahmed says you are free at four."

"Yes, certainly."

"Wonderful, see you later," and he hung up.

He was never one to use too many words, but it did leave me a little perplexed as to what I may have done wrong. All those guilt feelings I had back at the college resurfaced. I may have been calm and composed on the surface, but butterflies were never far from my stomach.

***

At the appointed time, I dutifully entered the secretarial office outside the Prof's room and three sets of eyes looked up to register it was me. Joanne looked up from her keyboard, smiled and nodded but it was Mrs Ahmed who just simply said, "You may go through now."

A quick knock and pushing the door open and I was within the air-conditioned office with low level lighting.

Professor J-P said, "Ah, here he is! Sit down Phil." I sat on the only chair available as three others were also in the room. Simon was there and two smartly dressed middle aged men I had never met before.

Prof J-P introduced the strangers as Les and Tony from the Municipal Engineers Office at the Borough Council. Typical of the Professor not to give surnames as he was always so casual and relaxed. He went on to explain that the department were proposing to expand the running of a few commercial courses for CPD (Continuous Professional Development) amongst both the private and public sectors. It was typical of our education sector to have so many acronyms. I used to say that education had TMA (Too many acronyms). My mind started playing silly little games again and I toyed with Special High Intensity Training (or SHIT) and Construction Regulations and Practice (or CRAP).

I came too quickly enough. The Professor's soft voice continued, "What we are thinking, Phil, Simon, is that you two might like to arrange a short course on building defects and how to identify them and design accordingly to avoid them."

When he said, 'you two might like to arrange' what he actually meant was 'you two will arrange'. You read between the lines very quickly. He went on to explain that I could look at the structural design whereas Simon could cover the material aspects.

We both agreed that it was a great idea but reading between the lines what we really meant was, 'Oh fucking hell, do we have to?'

The Prof went on to say that we could deliver the course as a one day seminar in-house or externally within the Greater Manchester region. Tony, who had been silent for the most part, explained that their engineers would also like to be brought up to date with the current design specifications, standards and regulations, and additionally, the advancement of modern-day materials available to the designers.

After the meeting, the Prof left the four of us to discuss this further over coffee and biscuits which Joanne had carried through to one of our meeting rooms. As we sat around idly chatting, I really felt as though I was starting to contribute to the work of the department and pushing the boundaries. In short, I felt relevant.

***

The chance encounter I had with the mysterious girl last term outside the kebab shop kept haunting me. On a couple of occasions during the first month of term I found myself driving around that area on my way back to David and Anna's house after leaving work. It was always after a late seminar session so it would have been about nine p.m. I wasn't sure why or what I was doing there, or what I was expecting, but it was like a magnet pulling me in. I was intrigued and fascinated but also wary and a little scared.

I did spot a couple of girls who may have been working the street, but I didn't want to stop or look too closely despite my own curiosity. Yet, I found myself turning the car around and driving the opposite way just for another chance to see them again, even if it was fleeting.

***

Simon had produced some fantastic slides and examples of materials which notoriously deteriorated by any of; thermal movement, over exposure to moisture, mortars that rehydrated, wetting and drying, rot, rust, concrete spall, frost damage, exposure to salts, excessive heat, etc. I was impressed.

For my own part I was collating a series of slides showing the effects of poor design in contributing to these conditions, inadequate movement joints in masonry panels (including coping stones), shrinkage of concrete during the curing process not having slip joints provided, inadequate cover to steel reinforcement for concrete, foundation movement from settlement and heave. I was grateful to John for providing me with some stuff on foundation design, including typical borehole logs, how to read them and how to establish suitable safe ground bearing pressures.

I had also produced an update on the changes made to the British Standards and how they influenced the Eurocodes. To be frank, there was not a great difference between them as most of the Eurocodes encapsulated our own trusted British Standards except the emphasis was on ultimate state rather than elastic design.

Within three weeks we had produced a series of four lectures, each lasting an hour, where we could present together and dovetail our ideas. I thought we could make a good comedy duo but who was going to be the straight guy?

The department's external liaison office was busy drumming up potential clients, and the idea was that we could either present this short course in our own lecture rooms, but ideally, in hotels and conference centres. It would look more professional to be away from the university, besides, we could get expenses.

We planned that we could start lecture 1 at ten a.m., lecture 2 at eleven thirty a.m., lecture 3 at two p.m. and the final one at three-thirty p.m., leaving thirty minutes Q and A time.

The only fly in the ointment was that department planned to deliver these on Fridays and Bella's premonition that I would be committed on Friday afternoons was coming true. At least it wasn't every Friday.

***

I was standing outside the church hall waiting for the Brownies to finish on Thursday evening and used the time sensibly by texting Bella. It was getting tougher for me to talk on the phone as I could never really say what I wanted, and I am sure it was the same the other way around too. It had got to the point where we were content with this arrangement. I would just text about my day, send my love to her and the boys, when I would be back and so on. It was devoid of any emotion apart from the obligatory 'X' at the end.

Jasmine and her friends bounced out of the hall looking for their parent or guardian (I assumed the latter).

Jasmine was clutching, not one, but two new badges; Mindfulness and Dancing, she was so delighted that she instinctively hugged me, which felt a little uncomfortable, especially as I was getting glances from some of the mothers who knew I was only the lodger. I smiled as kindly as I could and led Jasmine away but avoided holding her hand, well, not while we were in view of the others.

I opened the door (without ringing the bell), and Jasmine couldn't wait to tell Anna about her new badges. She wanted them sewn into her Brownie top straight away. Anna said she would do it that evening and thanked me for collecting her.

"I don't know what we would do without you." It was said with genuine warmth.

I couldn't help noticing she looked tired and David still wasn't back from work. The clinical trials had taken on huge significance apparently and the timings were critical.

That evening I wasn't particularly busy, so I offered to read Imogen a bedtime story. She offered me a myriad of books on Fairies, Ponies, Paddington Bear, Princesses and Hungry Caterpillars.

"Shall I tell you a story instead of reading a book?"

"Yes, please Uncle Phil," with real eagerness.

I told her the story of 'Barn on Fire' as I could remember almost word for word from my readings with Sebastian. It was a pity I didn't have the book to show her the illustrations but that didn't concern her, and she loved it.

"Another," she said when I had finished.

After a pause to recall another, I embarked on 'Pig Gets Stuck' and though I had to ad lib a little, I was able to tell her the story.

This time tomorrow, perhaps Sebastian will let me read to him.

***

It was staggering how quickly the term flies by. Easter was almost upon us, and I needed to draft final examination papers for my subject areas, have them moderated for content and validity and approved by the exam board. It was something I should have started to do a few weeks ago. Greg sat in the staff room smugly saying he'd done his soil mechanics paper weeks ago. I found an ally in Simon who admitted he hadn't started his either. Much later I discovered that Greg had only taken a paper he prepared two years earlier and changed all the numbers. Cheating bastard.

To be honest, I found writing the paper fun. I know my students wouldn't find it fun in any interpretation of the word, but all those examples I had delivered in my lectures I could combine and give little twists and tweaks to really test their knowledge. The Structural Design 1 paper was to be two hours long and they could answer four out of six questions. I was thinking that when I was an undergraduate, I had a three-hour paper and had to answer two questions from three. Students today don't know they're born.

Once I had started, it didn't take too long to do both the Structural Design 1 paper and the structural mechanics paper. I also had to make contributions to Structural Design 2 for the final year students as well. The thing that took the most time was the mark schemes, but I found a cunning way to solve my dilemma, I ran the designs through a computer programme by inputting all the design loads. The machine churned out all the salient bits of information, bending moment, shear forces, deflections, bearing stresses, beam sizes, reinforcement areas for concrete slabs, stability and torsion checks, etc. Once again, I thought of my undergraduate days, and this was all done by hand. Lecturers today don't know they're born either.

***

End of term was just a couple of weeks away and a strange thing happened to Greg. The phone rang in the staff room, and it was the manager of the local Barclays Bank branch just down the road. He asked if Greg had his Barclaycard with him. A quick check in his wallet confirmed it was indeed missing. The bank manager explained that it had been handed into the branch by a passer-by and had been sent back to Northampton for re-issue. The manager had put his mind at rest and said that the new card will be issued by Barclaycard and the replacement should be with him within five working days. A very relieved Greg was very grateful for the bank manager's call.

A week later he still had not got his new card, so he rang Barclaycard to find out what was happening only to discover his account had been spent to the maximum credit limit of six thousand pounds. The penny then dropped — it wasn't the bank manager that phoned but the thief himself. It was designed to prevent Greg from stopping his card before the thief could pilfer his account. The police believed the thief would have known about Greg, where he worked and how to contact him. If I recall correctly, Greg did get his money back from Barclaycard, but it was a salutary lesson to us all.

***

Back at home over Easter I was determined to do more with the boys. I was able to take Francis to cricket practice and he did play in some U15 matches against some other local village teams. In the three matches I was able to see him play, he only batted once but he did score five runs including a streaky boundary, but they all count. He did bowl in all three games though and was getting better each time. He took two wickets in his third match and jumped for joy when the ball crashed into the batter's stumps for his first and there was a catch for his second. Most of the time he ran around the field like a mad thing, but he was so keen.

Sebastian came along too but was not bothered about watching his big brother, instead he played on the swings, the rocking horse and finally the climbing frame before he turned his attention to some creepy crawlies in the grass.

Bella came to watch Francis in the games even though she knew little about cricket. She settled herself into a folding chair in front of the pavilion with a large floppy hat and wearing her oversized sunglasses. She knew three of the other mums and sat with them for the entire match drinking cordials from the bar. As a proud dad, I was patrolling the boundary rope and kept moving to find better vantage points, but to be honest, it made no difference where I stood. To this day, I still can't remember whether they won or lost the games, but it didn't matter.

It was a relaxed time as we did the usual things. We went over to Boston to see my dad once, met up with John a couple of times, sang in the choral group weekly but my heart wasn't in it, especially as they were working through some Gilbert and Sullivan productions.

We visited her parents at least twice a week, although I was not comfortable around her mum and dad. Her mum was all right with me but her dad could be a bit acerbic at times. I put this down to his ill health but he had been a bit of a tyrant when Bella was a young girl. Things were not easy when Bella was growing up as her mum had a miscarriage before she herself was born. Tragedy was to strike again when Bella was two years old, and her little brother was stillborn, and I am sure they never really came to terms with their losses. Nowadays, you would like to think that counselling services may be available, and they could confront their grief together.

Bella's father was of the old school, stiff upper lip, let's move on brigade and don't show any weaknesses. I am convinced that's why he turned to drink and there were many a time when we visited, he was half cut from whisky, even when we were courting. Like a lot of alcoholics, he denied there was a problem and he could disguise his state well in public, but if you knew him, it was obvious he'd been at the scotch.

Bella spoke little of her childhood and I was convinced that a lot of her problems stemmed from her father's dogmatic approach to parenting. He was very strict about homework, who she could and couldn't see, when she had to be back in the house each evening, what was acceptable to wear and so on. Makeup and jewellery were certainly not allowed.

Bella and I met, unsurprisingly, through the church but we were in different choirs. I was introduced to my choir when I was about eight or nine years old in Boston, whereas Bella started when she was about twelve in Louth. It just so happened that there was a music festival in Lincoln Cathedral and various choirs were all invited to take part. She was about seventeen when I first saw her. I was attracted by her long dark hair (although she has it shorter nowadays) and her small button nose, which suited her pale clear skin. That first glimpse of her was quite memorable, she looked quite wistful and serious as she stood, by pure chance, in a shaft of sunlight pouring through the clerestory windows of the Cathedral illuminating her like an angel. It was like a spotlight focussing on her alone. I am not particularly religious, despite my associations with church choirs, but this vision may have been designed by God himself, and who was I to argue.

I plucked up the courage to introduce myself and see if she would like to meet me again.

A few days later I arranged to pick her up and took her to see the film 'The Age of Innocence', although I was quite keen to see 'Pulp Fiction'. A more highbrow serious screening would be more appropriate for our first date I reasoned. As I write this now, I realise the significance of the film title as Bella was in an age of innocence, yet another metaphor I am assuming. Nevertheless, we seemed to get along really well from the beginning.

In those early days, Bella was very keen on seeing me and wanted more and more from our relationship. It was inevitable that we would get engaged, marry, buy a house, plan for children and settle into suburbia with such ease. For two and half years leading up to our wedding, the whole relationship felt like a juggernaut, and nothing was going to stop it. Looking back, it was not me with my foot on the accelerator, but equally I did nothing to apply the brakes.

I recognise all these years later that the appeal for Bella to leave her childhood home was probably greater than the love she felt for me. Cynically, I feel as though I had been the catalyst for her escape from that controlling household, and I admit, to feeling used.

***

Any private work John had put my way had dried up although we did a couple of little jobs while I was there that Easter. The first was a structural survey of a dilapidated house on the outskirts of North Hykeham. It had been left empty for the past three years and was subject to a planning application for either demolition or conversion into flats depending upon the report I would be submitting. The second job John had put my way was the setting out of a new steel framed agricultural building. As we were walking around the site, I wondered how John got these jobs.

"Ah," he said, "wheels within wheels."

I was no better informed but clearly, he had contacts in low places.

***

During the last week of the holiday period, we needed to buy Bella a new car as hers was becoming unreliable. I sold my Kawasaki motorbike for cash but kept the Honda 400 four which was left to me by Jerry's widow, Anya. I cleaned the Honda and got it started but it wasn't insured and didn't have an MOT. I started to wonder about the logistics of riding the bike to Manchester in the coming summer months. I knew I wouldn't do it though. It was a long journey for such an old bike, I would worry about breaking down, the traffic, parking it outside David and Anna's place, how would I carry my suitcase and briefcase? I admired people who have no concerns about climbing onto an old motorbike and going to the South of France for a week, but I am not one of those people.

I was born a worrier, not a warrior.

Chapter 8

Walking up the familiar uneven paving slabs on the first day back, I rang the bell and turned the key in the lock simultaneously.

"Hello, it's me, returned from the wilds of Lincolnshire!" I called expecting the girls to run down the corridor.

There was no answer and clearly, they were all out somewhere. It was about five p.m. and I made myself a mug of tea and waited for their return. I unpacked my things in the attic room, made the bed with the sheets and pillowcases left by Anna, cleaned the floor with the vacuum cleaner and went back down again to sit in the kitchen to await their return.

After an hour or so, the front door opened, and Anna appeared carrying Imogen. In turn, Imogen was carrying her teddy in her right arm but her left arm was in a sling. David and Jasmine came in and shut the door behind them.

David raised his eyebrows and gave out a sigh and Anna had certainly been traumatised by Imogen's accident.

"Oh, my. What's happened?" Was the best I could come up with.

"We've just come back from the hospital," Anna said in a weakened voice. "Imogen has a greenstick fracture of her wrist." She walked past me and disappeared into the lounge and allowed David to complete the story.

"She was standing on a park bench and was going to run and jump off but slipped. She ended up trapping her wrist under the armrest of the bench."

"Poor Imogen," I said. It was a pathetic response but what else can you say? I added, knowing the answer already. "Is there anything I can do to help?"

"No, thanks, but thank you, Phil."

Turning my attention to Jasmine. "Are you OK, munchkin?"

"Yes, thank you Uncle Phil. It was a bit scary."

"I'm sure it was sweetheart."

I offered to go to the local fish and chip shop, bought a massive number of sausages and chips and we ate them out of the paper with tomato sauce. It was very unhealthy but at least it was one less thing to worry about.

Later in the evening David said he needed to go back to work. It seemed rather tactless of him, as Anna, Jasmine, and especially, Imogen, were in need of some emotional support. The TV was on, but no one was paying much attention as Anna was asleep. Imogen was asleep on her lap and Jasmine had snuggled in beside Anna and had also fallen asleep. It had been a tough day. Anna looked so serene at that moment despite the trauma they had experienced and my heart went out to the three of them huddled together.

The last series of lectures I gave to the second-year students was on masonry design. It was not my favourite material as there wasn't a lot to it. You could only use masonry in compression, and of course, it has to be constructed vertically. The scope of design was limited to checking for crushing, stability and slenderness. In the programme I had allowed for the last two lectures to be on the subject but covered it in just one. This meant I was able to give a revision lecture for the final session and we recapped steel beams and columns. During that lecture, I was inundated with questions about what was going to be in the exam. I could give nothing away of course but pointed them in the direction of previous papers as a guide.

As they filed out at the end, several of them had the good grace to come and thank me personally for the programme of study. It brought those warm feelings of satisfaction I experienced back at Lincoln. It reaffirmed my belief that I had made the right decision to come here.

***

That evening I finished late again and inexplicably found myself driving back to that same area where that girl approached me all those months ago. This time I drove along a new street, and it was clearly in a rundown state. Rows of terraces all abutting the pavement, wheelie bins littered any convenient alcove, old newspapers lying in the gutters, satellite dishes mounted on a few walls; however, the most striking thing was the number of windows displaying a red glow. Some had red curtains with a bright light behind, others had standard lamps with red shades and some brazenly just had a bare red-light bulb hanging from a ceiling pendant. So, this is what a red-light district is, is it?

***

In bed that night I kept thinking about my discovery and vowed I would venture into the twilight, or more correctly, red-light zone at some stage in the future. Not sure when but I might.

***

The next evening, while it was still light, I drove to the same street and parked the car. I had only walked about twenty yards when a girl in an open doorway of the terraced houses asked if I was looking for business. It seemed like the stock phrase used by these women. She was young, twenty perhaps, and had the beauty that all young girls have.

"Hi, are you free to see me now?" It's hard to be casual in these circumstances.

We went in, agreed a fee for straight sex and almost immediately she settled on the sofa pulled down her knickers and rolled up her short skirt. After placing a condom on me I entered her and within seconds had exploded. While we were putting ourselves together afterwards, I started to notice how spartan the room was. A large sofa, small coffee table with the ubiquitous red lamp on top and a threadbare carpet. There may have been a few paintings or posters on the wall, but that was it.

Leaving was made easy but I wanted to thank her, perhaps invite her to dinner, ask for her phone number, go to the cinema with her, at least get to know her name. None of that was going to happen of course. I kissed my own fingertips and placed them on her lips to say, 'thank you'. It was the closest to any emotional involvement I could make.

Once back in the car I experienced an enormous feeling of relief and satisfaction. I knew then that I had turned a corner and coming back here was almost inevitable.

***

Back at the house, I went straight up to the attic room after checking everyone was OK. Imogen was still in some discomfort, but children always seem to recover quickly, even from a fracture. Anna still looked tired but content and Jasmine was in her room. David was not back from work. I wanted to hide away in the attic that evening as I wasn't proud of my recent liaison, and I felt quite ashamed but also strangely liberated. I couldn't look Anna in the eye,

I couldn't talk and play with the girls, and I couldn't talk to David, even if he had been there.

***

The following weekend was the same as all other weekends. We did venture into Lincoln to buy some cricket stuff for Francis. It seems a rite of passage for a father to buy his own son his first ever cricket bat. It wasn't just the bat though, he needed a helmet, gloves, pads and a box. Hopefully, I don't need to explain a cricket box but let's put it succinctly, boys need protection in a certain area. Francis was extremely embarrassed when I suggested he had one.

Bless him, he quietly wandered over to me and whispered. "OK, Dad, I'll have one."

***

Sunday evening, I had a chance to catch up with John. We went to the local pub, the 'King's Head', and had a couple of pints of 'Poacher's'.

"I'll tell you one thing, John, beer in Manchester is not as good as this."

"Oh, so there is some good in Lincoln then?"

"I do miss the place, you know." This needed more explanation, so I went on. "It's just that I seem to be leading two separate lives. Working in Manchester and home here in Lincoln."

"It was your choice."

"So, who told me about the advert for the job, who encouraged me to apply and said I would be daft not to accept it?" It was said with some jocularity.

"You'd always think 'what if?' had you turned it down."

"Yes, you're probably right. Another?"

***

The last two weeks of term after the students had left to go home was probably the busiest. I had a mountain of exam scripts to mark for Structural Mechanics, Structural Design 1 and half of Structural Design 2. I took myself off to an empty seminar room and worked through the piles in the most methodical way possible. I started with question 1 on all the scripts to avoid fluctuations of marks. The danger of marking the first paper from start to end, is that by the time you get to the last paper you realise you may have started harshly and then could become more lenient towards the end. I had to be disciplined. Even still, when you've marked the same question a hundred and twenty times it is something of a success to start question 2.

Simon and I also had to deliver our short course at the Victoria Hotel Conference Centre to the Borough Council's Building Control officers. It surprised both of us how many there were, we were expecting about fifteen to twenty but it was nearer fifty on the day. To be fair to Simon, he made the larger contribution to the lectures and his style complimented mine. He was precise and knowledgeable, and I admired him. He had, after all, acted as my 'buddy' or 'minder' during this first year and it couldn't have gone better.

My relationship with Simon was always professional, I tried to emulate his dress sense; a smart suit, shirt and tie were the rigueur, almost like a uniform. We made a point of not wearing the same tie on consecutive days, in fact I used to take at least five ties with me each week and rotate them from my wardrobe from home. Christmas and birthday presents often included a tie. Some of the staff at the university were scruffy beggars and you could tell who the 'lefties' were. It was not a case of being snobby or anything, it was a sense of pride in our presentation to students. I would not want to deliver a lecture to a hundred and twenty undergraduates in jogging bottoms, T-shirt and trainers.

I had collated all my exam scripts in rank order, arranged the project work alphabetically and presented my spreadsheet of marks, grades and recommendations ready for the exam board sitting the following afternoon. It would free me up to take Anna and Imogen to the Orthopaedic Clinic for Imogen's appointment later in the day as David was unable to take them.

***

We sat in clinic five for a good half hour before Imogen was called through. During that time, Imogen sat playing with the dolls and cars strewn on a play mat in front of us, demonstrating to anyone watching how resilient kids really are. Her temporary disability of her left arm did not hinder her as she manoeuvred the unrealistic scenario of a doll driving a Jaguar sports car.

"Are you all right, Anna?" I said.

"Thank you, yes, just a bit tired," she replied. After a few moments of silence she added. "Will you come in with us to see the Consultant?"

"If you want me to, I will."

"Yes, please. It's easier if there are two of us to understand and remember what the doctor says."

I still had trouble understanding why David wasn't sitting here instead of me. Surely, he would want to know what's going on. I would want to know if it was Francis or Sebastian. I certainly wasn't going to ask Anna that question though, she had enough to worry about.

A nurse called out, "Imogen Golding?"

"Please come with me Phil," implored Anna.

In the consulting room, Dr Jarvis invited us in and sat us down. He examined the X-rays Imogen had at the time of the accident and the ones taken just an hour earlier.

"You'll be pleased to know Imogen is making a good recovery," Dr Jarvis said with a smile and upbeat message. "The fracture has pretty much healed but I would like her to wear a protective arm brace for another two weeks. It can be taken off at bedtime and bath time but should be left on at all other times." He looked at me and said, "Is she sleeping well enough?"

Fortunately, Anna intervened and said she was and that her appetite hadn't been diminished. She had woken in the night a few times and called out for her mum.

"That's understandable and quite common," said Dr Jarvis. "Is she right-handed?"

"Yes," I said without thinking. Anna looked at me with a half-smile and half laugh. I felt I should apologise. "Sorry, I am not Imogen's father, but I do live with the family." I added in David's defence, "her father is involved in some important medical research and couldn't be here today."

Anna rescued me by giving some more information to Dr Jarvis. The doctor went on to say he did not feel it necessary to give Imogen any pain killers but as a precaution, if they were needed, he would furnish Anna with a prescription.   On the way back home in the car, Anna just said, "Thank you again, Phil. I really do mean it when I say it's good that you are around."

***

The exam board went relatively smoothly. It was chaired by the Prof, and he reminded us of the strict confidentiality of the proceedings. Each course tutor took it in turns to lead the discussion regarding their individual tutor group. There were a few failures in the first year sadly, of the intake of a hundred and fifteen students, three had left during the year and four failed the exams. Those four would be offered a chance to repeat the whole year but it was felt they should be advised not to do so unless there was a genuine desire to do better or there were mitigating circumstances. About a tenth of the cohort would be asked to resit at least one exam, but the majority had done well. The second-year students had all passed (apart from three students who needed resits in soil mechanics) so there were no resits required in Design 1 and it was the same story for the final year students too. I hadn't sat on such an esteemed examination board before; I had been involved in exam boards at college level of course but there was much more gravitas associated with proceedings here.

***

The following week, Simon and I presented another of our short courses this time to one of the local Construction Forums. The attendees were mainly from the private sector, estate agents, quantity surveyors, architects and even a landscape gardener (not sure how he got the email!).

***

During that last week there were several things I wanted to clarify. The few discussions I'd had with Bella suggested that she was not ready to move, if at all. She showed no interest in even wanting to visit Manchester, despite David and Anna's open invitation. During the whole academic year, she did not visit once. This uncertainty had delayed me looking for properties, even a studio flat, I was anxious that I may be overstaying my welcome with David and Anna. I needed to have that conversation with them soon. I also wanted to show my appreciation of their hospitality by taking them out for a meal. I knew the girls liked Italian food, so I found a nice restaurant, 'Carlo's', which was within walking distance from the house.

"Oh, we love Carlo's," said Anna when I suggested it and the girls whooped at the prospect.

***

Thursday was a good day as Brownies had finished for the summer and David was around so the five of us set out about five p.m. Imogen still had her arm brace but for the main part she was as back to normal as possible.

David and the girls were ahead of us and I turned to Anna and said, "Look, I want you to be honest with me. I don't want to be an imposition on you. It looks like Bella has no intention of moving and I should get myself a place of my own."

Before I could go on, Anna intervened. "We were wondering about Bella. If she is worried about the move, I could always talk to her."

"That's very thoughtful, but it's not you or me or Manchester. It's just she loves where she is and doesn't see why she should move."

Anna went on to say, "David has moved three times in the last ten years to different research clinics and as his wife, I've felt obliged to move with him. I didn't really have a say in the issue as David is very ambitious and has a strong drive to succeed. We were in Oxford to start with, then Aberdeen briefly, Lincoln and now here."

"Is that where you two met? Oxford?"

"Yes, he was doing his PhD when I was a fresher."

"Cradle snatcher!" I joked.

"Sorry," she said, "do I sound silly by saying I admired him for the important work he was doing?"

"Well, we are all attracted to start relationships for different reasons I guess."

I wanted to know more about how Anna felt about how her life had been shaped but now was not that time, besides, Anna brought the conversation back to what we had been discussing.

"Look, Phil, it really is not a problem if you want to stay with us next year. The girls would miss you if you were not here. They actually really like having you around." After a short pause she added, "just not at weekends." She laughed at her own little joke.

So, it was settled. I would be lodging with David and Anna next year and the status quo would continue. I knew Bella would be relieved at the prospect, but I am not sure if my boys would be so accepting of the situation. They did miss me during the week, but the weekends were always good enough.

I took a deep breath and pushed it out audibly. "Thank you, Anna. I would miss the girls too if I moved on."

I was looking forward to the Lasagne at Carlo's now combined with the entertaining prospect of watching Imogen struggle with one hand through her spaghetti.

***

The summer months went by as they always did; quickly, painlessly, seamlessly. The boys were now fourteen and seven and I could hardly believe that Francis was going into year ten starting his GCSE's. He'd picked some random subjects, but I had always advised him to pick the ones he enjoyed not the ones he felt he had to do. I remember as a kid choosing French and geography when I really wanted to do music and history. The only reason I chose them was the teachers were strict and they would make me work harder. I hated school. I think that's where I get my empathy for students who struggle as I had the bare minimum of qualifications when I left school. I, somehow, ended up at the age of sixteen working for a Consulting Engineer but didn't know what a consultant did. After going day release to college for five years to get my Ordinary National Certificate and then Higher National Certificate , I then went to Bristol University to study Civil Engineering.

I am sure my father had something to do with pushing me towards Consultant Engineering. I shall have to ask him sometime how that came about.

***

As it happens, we did not have a family holiday that year. I think because of all the remoteness of our relationship we never really planned anything. We ended up doing lots of days out to places like Alton Towers, Skegness, walks in the Lincolnshire Wolds and a day to watch the Test Match between England and New Zealand at Trent Bridge. Francis really enjoyed that day and wanted to go back the next day, but he settled for watching it on TV.

The time with Bella could only, sadly. be described as platonic. We went around like two weak North-seeking magnets, slightly repelling each other. Don't get me wrong, I wanted her, badly, I wanted to push her onto the bed and rip off her knickers and bury my face within her. Fantasy is so far removed from reality.

Chapter 9

Of course, I still had my key but as I walked up the rickety paving slabs (I'm sure they were worse than they were in June), I rang the bell and waited.

Anna was expecting me, but she sent Jasmine and Imogen to open the door.

"Good evening, I'm looking for two munchkins," I said. They both shrieked with delight. Imogen hugged me and Jasmine hugged both of us. Anna stood halfway along the corridor with that familiar and genuine smile. "How are things?" I said to her.

"Fine. Come on in. It's pizza again I'm afraid."

"I like pizza."

This is all so familiar.

***

Walking up the stairs from the back entrance in the engineering department, I was aware of the smell. It was floor polish just the same as always but being away from the place for a few months you forget the aromas.

I went first to the secretarial office where Joanne looked up from her keyboard, smiled and nodded. Even Mrs Ahmed acknowledged me. "Good morning, Mr Avery, welcome back."

At that moment I felt seven foot tall, full of oxygen, chest expanded and vibrant. I am really happy here I thought. "Thank you, Mrs Ahmed." I didn't know her first name.

I cleared my pigeonhole and was surprised at the quantity of paper that had been stuffed, not only in my pigeonhole, but everybody else's. Most of it was crap and I could deposit it in the recycling bin. I was looking for my timetable and relieved to see it was virtually the same as last year so at least I can travel on a Monday morning again instead of Sundays. There were a few alterations to my timetable. I now had the whole of Structural Design 2 as well as 1. There was also another module, Land Surveying but Structural Mechanics had been given to someone else. No problem, I loved teaching surveying and would need to get acquainted with the university's supply of levels, theodolites and Electronic Distance Measurement instruments.

The land surveying module will require me to take the students out to do practical work. I would need to find some projects around the campus to carry out level surveys, setting out exercises, traverses for 'Bowditch' corrections, etc. Great.

I was starting to feel involved and vital.

Opening the door to our little staff room I was not surprised to see Simon Ostler there, nor was I surprised to see that Greg wasn't there. It was good to catch up with Simon. Apparently, he and his wife (they have no children) went inter-railing across Eastern Europe and took in places like Ljubljana, Piran, Zagreb, Split and Dubrovnik.

I told him we went to Skegness for a day. It caused some merriment.

I was keen to make a start on the surveying module and arranged for one of the technicians to get me a key to the surveying storeroom and a copy of the inventory. I also wanted to know the procedure for booking out equipment and charging of the electronic instruments. I made a copy of the site plan of the campus and faculties before taking several walks around the green spaces and buildings to plot potential traverses that could be made and identify where we could do setting out of roads, bridges, drains, curves, etc.

***

The next day I looked more closely at the Structural Design 2 syllabus and thought this is going to be a real challenge as it included aspects like steel plate girders, prestressed and post tensioned concrete, steel portal frames, moment distributions. Big breath, I can do this, where did I put my Steel Designers Manual? Incidentally, my copy of the Steel Designers Manual was a Christmas present from my mum. When I was at Bristol University, she asked what I really wanted for Christmas. Guess what?

I had been a little sneaky last year. I found a really good diligent student with impeccable notes and photocopied the entire work we had covered. It would make good teaching material for this year, and I could refine it as we go along. To be fair, I was impressed at the way I had presented it. The first few lectures were how to assess loads on a structure. I had broken it down to dead load (the weights of the permanent parts of any building or structure), Live loads (the contents, furnishings, people, storage, etc) and Imposed loads (Wind etc.). Next was timber design as it was the easiest of the materials to start with.

I had produced massive amounts of material to get me started and I decided to do other things around the city. I had always thought I would watch Man City (definitely not United) and had tentatively thought of applying for a season ticket but with all the uncertainty with Bella, had done nothing about it. As it happened Stockport County were at home to Lincoln City in a mid-week fixture on the Tuesday evening so I went on my own to see the game. It was drab and boring, and I found it difficult to show any allegiance to either side. It finished 2-0 to the County. None of that mattered as I walked away from the ground with five or six thousand others. No one there knew me, no one knew where I was and I was, surprisingly, very happy.

***

It was going to happen sooner or later, but the timing surprised me. It was week two of term and the students were still not back. I found myself leaving the department and took a diversion to drive to the street I found last term. It was still light but there was an overcast sky and it threatened rain, but it was still dry. I had decided I would not park in the street as before, because fundamentally I wasn't comfortable doing this, but I just wanted to look around again. There were indeed several girls in tight fitting and revealing clothes walking casually along the street. I passed them all by and was about to turn left back onto the main road to complete my journey unfulfilled, when I saw her. She was tall with dark ebony skin that shone, even in this drab light, she reminded me of a gazelle for some strange reason. I stopped the car and wound down the window.

She leaned in through the car window and said, "Hi honey. Are you looking for some fun?"

Her face was as beautiful as the rest of her and with such tight clothes you could certainly make out the rest of her. I said something inane like 'yes, please' and she slid in so gracefully. Now, I didn't know what to do as this scenario hadn't played out in my head before. I need not worry as she took complete control and directed me to a secluded block of garages. She gave a rundown of her prices and things she would do and things she would not do. We agreed on oral and I paid her the money which she slipped expertly into her clutch bag.

Almost mechanically, she reached over and took me out from my trouser after I had released my belt, she expertly covered me with a sheath that had mysteriously appeared from nowhere and went down on me. It may have been mechanical for her, but it sent little electric shocks through me. That initial contact made me gasp with pleasure and she knew it, she worked me so skilfully and it was over in just a few minutes, as announced by my feral boar groan.

Afterwards, I drove her back to the same spot where we met, and she slid out of the car with just as much grace as she had entered and slipped away to find another client. I could not help myself from watching her beautiful body move away with such elegance and warm shards of satisfaction were engulfing me.

***

Later, I had mixed feelings which ranged from pure satisfaction to one of complete shame. I returned to the house and disappeared into the attic room and didn't surface until the morning. As I got into the car to go to work, the wrapper of the sheath she had used lay discarded on the floor of the passenger well, fortunately the sheath itself had been discarded, presumably, somewhere around the garages. I chastised myself to think that wrapper may have been discovered by Bella, the boys, the girls or, even, Anna. I could have been taking the girls to school in the car this morning. What the fuck was I thinking?

***

The next weekend, Lincoln City were playing at home to Exeter City. I told Francis how I had seen Lincoln playing in Stockport the week before. It re-awoke his desire to go and see football again so we decided we would go. This time, Sebastian wanted to come too. I was hoping Bella may come but she just said, "You boys go and have a good afternoon, but don't give them pasties at half time."

"Are you sure you won't come?" I said. It was a nudge too much.

"I've had them all week. You don't know what that's like do you?" It was barbed and another shot across the bows.

***

Followers of football clubs; the fans (which of course is a derivation of the word fanatic) can be so tribal. I made sure we had seats in the family enclosure but even still the chants were clear and unmistakeable. 'Who's the wanker in the black' was one that started up when the referee gave a dubious decision to the Grecians (I know, I am just as bad knowing the nicknames but when you were a kid, footie magazines were a staple diet even then). At one point towards the end of the half, one of the Exeter players stayed down after a heavy challenge. You would expect the fans to be caring and considerate, wouldn't you? Not a chance, within a few seconds the home fans started chanting 'You're going home in a fucking ambulance'. I despair sometimes. I was just hoping that neither boy asked me to explain what the chanting was about.

To deflect any such conversation, I said, "Right, who wants a pasty?"

***

I phoned my dad the next day to see how he was. He was fine of course; these old country boys are tough. It was good to talk to him though and I told him about my new timetable, which now included all the structural design modules plus the land surveying unit. He showed some real interest and wanted to know more about the number of students I was teaching and whether I was a tutor to any of them.

Before he hung up, he made a point of saying, "But how are you really son?" I couldn't answer that, could I?

"No, I'm really good Dad, really enjoying the job, couldn't be better."

***

Thursday came around again, and I offered to take Jasmine to Brownies once more. Anna, I think, was slightly annoyed that David was not around to take more responsibility for his daughters as she made some comment like 'David should have been back by now'. It wasn't said in a way that particularly showed concern for him but more of exasperation.

"It's not a problem for me, really, I am happy to do so."

"Thanks Phil."

"Can I get anything while I am out?"

"Oh, yes, we need milk, bread and fruit juice." She was fumbling for her purse to look for some cash.

"It's OK, I can sort this."

Taking Jasmine by the hand we headed to the church hall and I would go on to the mini mart around the corner. A text message to Bella and then a phone call to John as he had left a message earlier in the day.

"Hi, John, how's it going?"

"Fine, Phil, are you back this weekend?" He knew I was.

"Yes, absolutely. I've no plans."

"Great, we need some steel beams designing for Langton's". Langton's was a small builder we had worked for before. We arranged to meet at eleven a.m. on Saturday.

Arriving back after Brownies, Anna had produced a Macaroni Cheese and the smell permeated the house and made everything so homely. Anna served David's portion on a plate for when he got back and dished up for the rest of us. The girls had plenty to talk about and it was entertaining to listen to them talk about My Little Pony and Fairy Princess stories.

Later, when I was working in my room, I could make out Anna practising her singing in the lounge. The girls were already tucked up in bed and fast asleep. I went to my bedroom door and opened it further so as to listen to her, but I could only just hear her as presumably she had the lounge door shut. As her voice floated up the stairwell it reminded me of Bella, but somehow Anna's singing seemed purer, gentler somehow. She started with a series of vocal exercises and then I was aware she was singing 'Jesu, Joy of Man's Desiring' by Bach. Whatever work I had planned to do that evening just stopped and I was aware that tears had materialised and were running down my cheeks. I imagined her in a long white dress singing on her own in a Concert Hall. David was indeed a lucky man.

***

Saturday morning, John rang to say he would be later than planned and hoped to be with us before one p.m. As the time slipped by it was getting close to one and Bella wanted to serve lunch. The boys were getting hungry.

"We can invite John to join us for lunch, can't we?" I said.

"Yes, but I don't want to be eating when he arrives."

It was now past one now, so I felt I could phone him and see where he was. Just as I was looking for my phone, he rang the doorbell.

"Come in John, you are just in time for lunch," I said.

"Sorry, sorry boys, sorry Bella, I don't want to impose."

Bella sat him down at the table along with the boys and the two of us. It was only pitta breads, carrot and cucumber stick with various dips and apple or orange juice, so nothing to fret about spoiling. It was clear to me from John's agitated state that he wasn't himself. Bella hadn't picked up on this and she was asking him questions about his work, Maria, his car and their holiday. Just mundane chit-chat really. The yoghurts came out of the fridge afterwards and I knew Francis and Sebastian would fight for the peach one.

After lunch, I took John to my study room upstairs on the pretence of looking at the Langton's project.

"Sorry, Phil, I left them in the car, I'll just fetch them."

When he came back in, Bella had made us coffee to take upstairs. When the two of us were together again I wanted to know what was troubling him.

"Are you all right John?"

"Sure, just a bit stressed."

"Fuck off, you're never stressed."

He looked up at me quickly and then looked down again before puffing out his cheeks with a grimace. I'd never seen him like this before. Apparently, Maria and he had decided to separate but they couldn't afford to sell the house and split the profits, there just wasn't enough equity to release. They had then decided to live separate lives but in the matrimonial home, Maria at one end and John at the other. Free to see anyone else they wanted. Although they had both found other short-term relationships it was always away from the house, that was until last night. Maria brought a man home, and they were sleeping together in what was originally John and Maria's main bedroom.

"I couldn't bear it," John said. "I got into the car at midnight and drove out into the Wolds and slept there."

"In the car?"

"Yes," he said.

"Oh, John, I'm so sorry."

I wanted to tell him about my night on the dunes near The Wash, but this was not an appropriate time.

"I'll be all right. I need time and space to sort myself out and I did agree to all of this so I can't blame anyone else but myself."

"Did you meet him?" I said unwittingly.

"Yes briefly, he was a fat bastard with thinning hair."

I started to smile, then snigger, tried not to laugh but then laughed out loud. John looked at me in horror to begin with, then broke into laughter too. We both laughed so much that tears were rolling down our faces.

Bella came upstairs to see what all the commotion was about. "Are you two OK?"

"Yes, Bella, but what did you put in that coffee?" That just started us off again.

Within an hour John had got his composure and resolve back and he was his old self once more.

"I'm going to find myself a bird and take her back to stay one night. I just hope she's a really loud moaner." That triggered another bout of laughter. Humour really is the best medicine.

***

The week three lecture for Structural Design 1 was the first on timber design. The hundred and ten or so second-year students had their 'Extracts' book open on page 126 and I was explaining how timber behaves in flexure and bending.

I had told them that floor joists can have various factors applied, including the depth factor. My delivery went something like.

"So, I want you to imagine a seven-inch-deep timber beam compared to, say, a nine-inch-deep beam, the stresses will vary due to the non-homogenous nature of timber…"

I tailed off because a student in the second row had a hand up. Now it's bad form to ask a question in a lecture, you should wait until the seminars afterwards to sort out those problems. I looked at him and invited him to speak.

With heavy sarcasm he said, "Mr Avery, what is an inch?"

Now at this point I should have engaged my brain but sadly I didn't do so in time.

"Well, drop your trousers and we'll find out."

Now I have had laughter in my lessons and lectures before, but this was on another scale. The students were literally rolling around the benches almost uncontrollable for a good five minutes.

For my part I was delighted at the witticism but equally horrified at what repercussions would come from this. There were several girls in the group too and I hoped no one took offence. One complaint could bring me into serious trouble, more than I ever faced at Lincoln, and I could be in danger of losing the one job I really love.

When eventually some order resumed, I apologised and said that I should indeed be using metric measurements. Old habits die hard was my plea for forgiveness.

I never breathed a word of this to anyone, and I mean anyone, for fear that I may get a phone call from Prof J-P. What would he say? 'Come and see me dear boy, we need an important chat'. Fortunately, no phone call was made to me.

***

About a week or two later, I arrived back at the house after work and Anna was sitting having tea with a friend.

"Hello Phil. This is Katie."

Katie had dark ebony skin which seemed to glow even in this natural light. She reminded me of my gazelle from the streets I met some weeks ago, but not as tall nor toned, but attractive nonetheless with a round face and perfectly round spectacles. I wanted to call her 'bubbles'.

"Hello Katie, pleased to meet you."

Anna explained that Katie lived not that far away and was a receptionist at Jasmine's school. She told Katie that I lecture in structures at the university and live in Lincoln, but lodging with them during the week.

I didn't want to interrupt their conversation, so I politely made my apologies and went up to my attic room to carry on working.

***

After the students had collected the various pieces of surveying equipment, they made their way down to the rear entrance of the departmental building. They had already been allocated groups and tasks for this week and I arranged they would all be doing the same tasks but in a round robin exercise over the next three weeks.

Group 1 were doing a theodolite traverse. Group 2, a level survey around the car park and student union building. Group 3 were doing a setting out exercise on the green and Group 4 were setting out curves.

Each task was designed to take two hours each but their inexperience caused some of them to overrun. Personally, I found it tough going from group to group to help them and thought there must be an easier way in future.

As the last group were making their way up the stairs again carrying all the equipment back to the store cupboards, the fire alarm sounded and the whole building had to be evacuated. Several hundred people were having to stand in the car park. In the distance we could hear multiple fire engines getting closer and closer. After thirty minutes the problem was identified as a false alarm caused by a Break Glass Fire Panel being broken by a surveyor's ranging rod. The culpable student didn't live that down for a long while. Mind you, I was not in their good books either when I discovered that a false fire alarm resulted in the university, or rather the departmental budget, having to pay a five hundred pound fine.

"Can I ask you a favour Phil?" said Anna.

"Sure."

"Do you think you can give Katie some structural advice for her house?" Anna went on to explain, "Katie's house is a modern terraced house and not very big. Katie wants to extend into the loft but she's not sure if it can be done and doesn't want to spend large amounts of money to get a surveyor's report if all they are going to say is it is not possible."

I was of course happy to help. Anna went on to say she herself would pay me whatever fee I deemed appropriate as Katie did not have a lot of spare cash presently. I assured her it wasn't a problem, as I quite enjoy helping.

I had some spare time that evening and so I walked round to Katie's place as it was only about three or four hundred yards. I rang the bell and Katie answered.

"Oh, thank you Phil. Do you mind doing this? I am ever so grateful for you having a look for me."

It really wasn't a problem. I looked in the loft and the roof construction was just as I suspected, a modern gang nail truss arrangement. There would be sufficient head room height, even with new floor joists to strengthen the existing ceiling joists. There would be an option of placing dormer windows to either the front or rear depending upon planning consent. The biggest problem would be access but I told Katie about a staircase that conforms to Building

Regulations but can be made to be quite steep. It would certainly fit in the space. The roof would need structural purlins which could either be ply box beams or steel.

Before I left, I made a few sketches of the sort of things I was thinking of.

Katie was very grateful and insisted I stay and share a bottle of wine with her. I didn't have the heart to say I wasn't keen on wine. She also produced a couple of bowls of nuts and mini cheddar biscuits.

To be honest, it was nice to talk to someone new. Someone who didn't know my background and would not have preconceived ideas of me.

In the next hour, we just chatted freely as she was very easy to talk to. I was able to tell her a few things about my life and I discovered, among other things, her parents were from the Caribbean originally. She was divorced, no children, her mother was quite frail, and Katie wanted to have her parents living with her, she is a school receptionist (but I knew that already) and she had three brothers who had all moved away from Manchester. This girl could talk for Jamaica!

Anxious to get back I said I must get going and if she needed anything else, let me know. My last piece of advice was to get a builder in for a free quotation based on the sketches I had given her.

At the door she took both my hands and pushed them together with her own and thanked me again.

After I let myself back in, Anna smiled her warmest smile, moved her head to one side and said,

"Thank you for doing that, I know Katie would be so appreciative."

***

News of my little witticism a few weeks ago had permeated amongst the student body, but fortunately, not amongst the staff. I discovered this one afternoon when a final year student, Liam, needed help with his dissertation. He was researching underpinning techniques suitable for a nineteenth century cottage. I was able to give him some advice, but he would need to establish the type of soil and strata below the building. He could glean this off a geological map probably.

"Most soils, Liam, are capable of taking about a tonne and a half per square foot."

Liam smiled and said with mock sarcasm. "What is a foot, Mr Avery?"

I couldn't help myself. "Allow me to drop my trousers."

Chapter 10

There was a time when I looked forward to weekends back in Lincoln. The drive over the Pennines, usually on the A57, but I did experiment with other routes, were relaxing and formed a natural break with, what I can only refer to, as my developing a schizophrenic lifestyle. In the past few weeks though I started to be aware of a slight dread of what might happen in the two or three days back home.

It was not that Bella was hostile, far from it, she would welcome me home with a cup of tea and a slice of Bakewell tart or a Belgian bun. To my mind, the welcome home would have been suitable for a brother or a friend but not a spouse. There may have been a perfunctory kiss on the cheek or a squeeze of the arm but nothing else.

It was good to see the boys though and that's what was important. Saturdays we had started watching Lincoln City, if they were playing at home, or kick about on the recreation ground. I helped Francis, when he would let me, with his physics, maths or chemistry and I enjoyed painting and drawing with Sebastian. Not so keen on Sebastian's recorder playing though.

It was noticeable that the routine for Bella and me to get ready for bed had changed. Bella would have a bath with the door locked, come out in a nightgown, read a book, turn out the light, and presumably, fall asleep within seconds with her back to me or a large portion of the duvet wedged between us. I would like to tell you about the mornings, but I never knew what happened as she was often up before me, dressed and organising breakfast. I was a heavy sleeper and not that great in the mornings. There were many a time Francis and/or Sebastian used me as a human trampoline as I came out of my stupor.

***

After one such weekend I was driving back to Manchester on the Monday morning with differing emotions. I was actually looking forward to seeing my students and going back to Anna and her girls. As an engineer I should be able to logically process all of this and come to a conclusion, but when has emotion ever been logical?

"I hope you don't mind, Phil." Anna said, "But Katie would be ever so grateful if you have some time to see her this week."

"I could probably make Wednesday if that suits her."

"I will tell her when I drop Jasmine at school. Are you sure you don't mind? It is an imposition I know but she does value your opinion."

Katie had apparently contacted two builders and they both came up with differing schemes and totally different estimates from what she expected. I really didn't mind as she was so easy to talk to and there was no pressure on either of us.

***

On Wednesday, I rang the bell outside and she greeted me with relief.

"Oh, Phil, you are so kind. Thank you."

She asked me in, and I took a seat on the sofa. Her front door led straight into her lounge and there was not a lot of space. I could quite understand her desire to expand somehow.

"Can I get you a drink?"

"Water is fine, thanks."

"I've bought some beer, if you'd prefer."

"No, water is good for me."

"How about a squash? Nibbles?" She was so anxious to please.

"I'm fine, really."

To appease her I settled on summer fruits squash and settled back to look at what these 'rogue builders' were up to. Having had time in the industry and keeping contact with my good friend John, you get to spot all the little tricks of the trades.

One of the schemes was ridiculous as the builder wanted to remove the entire roof covering and insert steel beams between the party walls. This would necessitate putting a 'top hat' arrangement (scaffolding over the whole house with metal sheeting to keep everything dry during the building work). No wonder that was going to be so expensive.

The other scheme was somehow worse, as they had failed to recognise that the floor needed strengthening and where they had proposed dormer windows, they would need planning permission. They also wanted to make one of the existing bedrooms much smaller to insert a traditional staircase instead of the one that I had suggested.

I apologised to Katie for inadvertently causing her any stress with this. She was aghast that I felt it necessary to apologise and she said she should be apologising to me. We agreed not to blame ourselves.

"Look, I'll tell you what," I said. "Let me come up with a drawing and specification and we will get three fairly priced quotes."

"Would you? Thank you. I will need to pay you though. How much would it be?"

I really didn't want to be paid. It would be a pleasure to get involved, after all, not surprisingly with what he's had to contend with, John had put little extra work my way recently.

I told her to leave it with me for a couple of weeks, I'll try and do it before the Christmas break, but if not, in the New Year. I did have that beer later and we talked for another hour or so before I made my excuses and left to go back to Anna's. We did decide that we would go out for dinner sometime soon though.

***

It had been a couple of months since the encounter with my gazelle. I had resisted the desire to visit the area as I felt quite depressed about the possible repercussions of that event. The human spirit can only endure so much though. I had avoided making dates with anyone in the Manchester area for so many reasons; Bella, lodging with Anna, the potential complications that would inevitably arise, adjusting to the area and my work at the engineering department. I could always find counter arguments.

Parking the car close to the same spot all those months ago, I was wondering if she still worked here. I passed a couple of open doorways, each occupied by a scantily clad girl beckoning me in, but I resisted. As I walked on, my heart beat a little faster when I saw that she was indeed still here.

"Are you looking for a good time?" she asked.

We went in and I hoped she may remember me, but of course she plainly didn't. Was I just another punter? I sincerely hoped I wasn't.

"What would you like? Hand, oral or straight sex." Well, she was straight to the point then.

"How much is it for everything, I mean full strip and a bit of everything?"

The price doubled but what the hell. We both took off our clothes and I still thought how pretty she was. It was the first time I had seen her breasts and they were small with pink nipples jutting out teasingly. I also noticed she had shaved her pubic hair. I found myself questioning why she was doing this.

She played with me for a while then started to suck on me as I caressed her breasts. After a few minutes she covered me with a sheath (where did that come from? It was like a conjurer's trick). She sat back open legged on the sofa, and I wanted to kiss her thighs and caress her, move up to her vagina and lick her passionately but she avoided all of that by taking me and guiding me into her. I moved slowly back and forth hoping she was enjoying this as much as me. I fondled her breasts again, stroked her legs, bent forward to kiss her nipples and the nape of her neck. At that point she stiffened and turned her head away to avoid another kissing situation. Then came a series of loud knocks on the other side of her front door.

"Come back in five minutes!" she shouted and then turned to me. "Are you finished yet?"

In one crushing second, I was finished. A mixture of anger, frustration, disappointment and impotence cursed through my body. I stood up, pulled off the condom and dropped it to the floor, dressed rapidly and left with hardly another word to her.

Instead of going back to the car, I walked in the opposite direction deeper into the street, not knowing where and what I was going to do, trying to resolve these massive emotions swirling around inside me. I was almost in tears, and they could have been tears of anger, tears of frustration, tears of depression, tears of self-pity. It was almost the same red mist that befell me when Bella said, 'have a wank in the bathroom'. On that occasion I could find sanctuary in the dunes but here I was in a concrete jungle, and this was not my territory.

"Are you looking for some fun?" said a sweet young thing from yet another doorway.

"Yes."

I held my composure long enough to agree to have straight sex in the doggy-style position with her kneeling on the floor. I pushed roughly into her. Her bottom was so smooth, white and beautiful but I took her by the hips and fucked her ferociously for several minutes before giving out that feral roar.

While dressing I apologised for being rough with her but could not begin to explain the circumstances.

"Don't worry about it," she said sweetly. "I'm used to it."

I made a point of kissing her cheek and genuinely thanking her. I slipped her another ten pounds and asked her to get something for herself.

As an engineer, I am supposed to be logical and clever. How the hell did I really expect a common prostitute to give me the love I really craved?

**

Back in my staff room I was a million miles from what happened yesterday evening. It had been a real contrast from last night to this morning. I had got back to Anna's late and went straight to my little self-imposed prison in the attic full of remorse and recriminations. This morning I felt better about myself, breakfasted and went swimming. Now I felt refreshed.

I was due to start a lecture at nine a.m. for Structural Design 2 on prestressed and post tensioned concrete. If I was prestressed last night I am certainly relaxed now.

**

If you set large projects for students to do, then you must expect to spend a long time assessing and processing them. I had such grandiose plans originally to design individual projects to avoid students collaborating with each other and submitting identical scripts for me to mark. To this end, I came up with an ingenious scheme where the students had to design a mezzanine floor set within an existing factory capable of being either used as storage, an office or a rest area. It was then further complicated by stanchions being placed at different centres, differing span beams, differing types of floor. When all these combinations were taken into account it produced a hundred and twenty differing design scenarios. That meant that every student had a unique design to produce and plagiarism, or as I like to call it, cheating, would be avoided.

The trouble with creating this monstrosity, is that I had to refer to my chart to see which student had which parameters so that I could mark accordingly. I was never, going to do this again because the last two weeks of term saw me sitting in the attic room night after night, like a hermit, covered by my duvet and wearing mittens and a hat as it was so cold.

Perhaps I wasn't so clever after all.

***

Christmas and New Year were not dissimilar from last year's festivities except we had Bella's mum and dad and my dad at ours on Christmas Day. We went to church for Midnight Mass on Christmas Eve and Bella sang in the choir. I declined the invitation to sing with them saying I would sit with Francis in the Nave (Sebastian was at home with Bella's mum and dad). It was a weird feeling that came over me during that Service, I had a premonition that this may be the last time I was going to be here. I don't mean I was envisaging my death, but internally prophesied that things will be changing. Things could not go on indefinitely like they have been. The feeling passed once outside the church but there was something gnawing away at me.

***

Driving back to Manchester on that first day after the holiday was quite treacherous. There had been snow three or four days earlier, thaw and then freezing over the last few nights. Bella thought it unwise to drive but I felt I had to get back as I had a lecture at eleven a.m.

As it happens, she was right, the A57 was blocked with traffic, and I was crawling along at a snail's pace. I had telephoned ahead so the department knew what the situation was, and they suggested that I turn around as most lectures had been cancelled and other staff couldn't get in either.

It was typical of me to soldier on regardless, the thought of repeating all this tomorrow would be a nightmare so let's get it over and done with.

Despite having left at seven a.m. I eventually arrived in Manchester at two-thirty p.m. There was no point heading to the department now so I headed to Anna's instead. It will be nice to see the munchkins and they can tell me all about their presents. I could then tell them about Francis and Sebastian's presents but it was unlikely they'd be that interested.

I did phone Bella to say I had arrived safely. I think she said something like. "Well done," and that was about it.

***

I rang the bell, turned the key and let myself in. The girls were there as their schools had closed due to bad weather, David too had been snowbound and the four of them were playing 'Uno'. The game was a Christmas present to Jasmine. The nice thing about 'Uno' is that there is no limit to how many people could play. The girls were keen for me to join in and so the five of us spent a very happy hour and a half playing the game as the dark evening drew in outside.

Anna had prepared a stew with dumplings. I could make dumplings really well as my mum taught me many years ago. The secret was to trap as much air into the flour and suet mixture by constant folding and kneading. I was going to offer but I knew what Anna would say.

It was good to be back, but I missed the boys. I made a point of phoning in the evening to talk to them before they went to bed, but kids don't want to talk on the phone for long, it just left me feeling a bit empty when I hung up.

Anna phoned Katie to say I was back, and I had cobbled something together for the loft extension. We arranged that I would pop round on the Wednesday evening.

***

"Hi Katie," I said as she opened the door.

"Come in, come in, it's too cold out there."

She made a vast cafetière of coffee and we sat talking about Christmas and New Year for a while. She had been at her parents for pretty much all of the festive period. Eventually I showed her my plans and specifications for the loft. She struggled to understand the jargon and found it difficult to read the drawings, but generally she liked the concept and the space it may create.

"We'll just need to find a few builders that may be suitable to approach," I said.

"Some people down the road have had building work done, do you think I could ask them for their details?"

"Absolutely, but make sure they would recommend them." I added with more caution than necessary.

We planned to go out for dinner one day next week as she was keen to repay me with something and I think she would appreciate the company and I certainly would.

"Carlo's?" I suggested.

"Carlo's," she agreed.

I was quite surprised that the clock was now approaching ten.

"Sorry, I must get back to see Anna," adding after too long a pause, "oh, and David, the girls will have gone to bed by now."

Was that a 'Freudian' slip?' I thought as I walked back. Clearly, I had spent more time with Anna than David since staying with them. David had spent a considerable number of evenings, and I gather weekends, away from home working. I was always impressed at his commitment, energy and devotion he gave to this vital research. Doctors and clinicians deserve every respect and admiration from the rest of us. I only hope he values Anna too, she deserves true love.

***

As I have mentioned before, I only ate at the university campus when I was working late or had seminars in the evening, so it was a rarity to go to the dining hall for food.

This particular day Greg joined me and as we were walking across the campus, I spotted someone familiar.

"Hello, young Alex," I said to one of my old tutor group from Lincoln.

A complete shock came over him and for a moment he looked at me unknowingly. Then there was a moment of recognition.

"Phil! Sorry, I mean, Mr Avery, how are you? What a surprise."

"I am happy to be called Phil, Alex. Good to see you dear boy." Was I turning into Prof J-P?

We couldn't talk for long because he was heading to a lecture. Greg had already walked on, and I would catch up with him later.

In the few moments we had he told me he had enrolled at the School of Architecture, and it was his first year there. He told me about some of the other lads, Dan was doing Quantity Surveying in Birmingham, James and Ollie were both at London doing, he thought, Building Surveying but couldn't remember exactly.

I gave Alex my extension number at the department or he could leave me a note in my pigeon hole and we could catch up later.

As we were about to leave and go our separate ways he said, "I really want to thank you Mr Avery, sorry, Phil, you really were a brilliant tutor and we appreciated everything you did for us, especially defending us at the disciplinary meeting."

There are some things money can never buy. This is one of those moments when you can justifiably feel proud to know you made a difference. Where would Dan and Alex be now if they had been thrown off the course at Lincoln following that 'Jack Daniels' episode?

***

"Table for two please?"

The waiter at Carlo's led us to a little cubicle near the back of the restaurant. It wasn't such a good table as when I brought Anna and the family, but it was comfortable enough. There were few people in as it was only six p.m. and I was intent on getting some marking done later in the evening.

Katie wore a blue dress, and it was the first time I had seen her out of her usual casual tank tops and slacks. I was still wearing my boring suit but had at least dispensed with the tie. Were the waiters curious about us? After all I was fifteen years older than Katie, she was a beautiful Jamaican, and I was a boring middle class white guy. Then I said to myself, people are not judgemental these days.

Being a creature of habit, I ordered a lasagne, and she went for a carbonara. I always avoid ordering spaghetti in public as I can never eat it with any decorum. I think Katie had some white sparkling wine, but I tried some of their Italian beer. It was a bit gassy but refreshing, nonetheless.

Our conversation went along without many hesitations as Katie was keen to talk about so many things;

the weather, my work, her school, her parents, my dad, my boys, Lincoln and Bella. I didn't intend to be indiscrete but with Katie you got the distinct impression you could tell her anything in confidence. It wasn't the beer talking as I had kept a clear head. I told her about the problems Bella and I were going through and she could empathise as she had an awful time with her ex-husband, Nathaniel. From all accounts he sounded as though he had been quite manipulative and controlling. It took her two or three years to get out of that marriage combined with a lot of counselling too.

I recounted the session we had had with the kindly face in Lincoln. It made Katie laugh and she placed her hand over her mouth and gasped.

"No? Really?"

I knew that she wanted to pay for the meal, to say thank you for the work I had done, but call me old fashioned, I found that uncomfortable. I insisted on paying and told her it was brilliant to be able to off load on someone willing to listen without judgement.

Back at her house she insisted I come in for coffee, but I was reluctant as I needed to mark some scripts and I was keen to get back and see Anna. It was only eight-thirty p.m., so I thought 'why not?'

'Why not?' indeed.

As soon as the front door closed, she pushed me back against the door and kissed me fully on the lips and cradled my head in her hands.

When I came up for air, I said, "Katie."

"It's OK," she said finding my belt and undoing it. "It's OK," she repeated while undoing my trouser and releasing me. For the third time she said, "It's OK, I want you to be relaxed." She sank to the floor and placed me in her mouth, within seconds I was hard. I certainly wasn't expecting this, and I also know I wasn't ready for another relationship. But then, hell, I am only a man.

I let her suck on me for a while then lifted her off the floor and pushed her onto the sofa. We kissed passionately and I tried to remember how her dress might come off. I only managed to get the top half down, removed her bra to expose a pair of beautiful ebony breasts. They were much bigger than I imagined when she was fully dressed, and I licked her nipples while sliding my hand into her panties and allowing my fingers to explore inside her. My brain was reminding me not to fuck her although my little brain was saying 'go on, fuck her', I wasn't ready for that and I overruled my little brain. Instead, I pushed her head down on me again and waited to hear 'welcome to Kings Cross' combined with my feral boar cry.

Afterwards, we lay for a while cuddled on the sofa and I tried to avoid dozing off altogether. I am sure she was hoping I would stay the night but my heart was saying I needed to get back to see Anna and retire to my attic room.

"I'm very sorry, Katie, I will need to get going." It was lame of me.

"Won't you stay? Please?"

"I ought to get back otherwise it will be difficult to explain to the girls in the morning." Reading between the lines I meant 'it will be difficult to explain to Anna'. I went on. "Plus, I have essential work to do tonight and my clothes are back at Anna's."

"You could always head back early in the morning."

"I'm sorry, if I knew that was going to happen between us this evening it might have been different. Sorry."

She reluctantly agreed and I continued making my excuses, kissed her passionately and held her tightly for longer than I thought necessary.

Walking back to Anna's house, I thought, 'what the bloody hell am I going to do now?'

Chapter 11

The weekend back in Lincoln was a difficult time as Bella
had wanted the house decorated for ages and I had done
nothing about it. I was convinced we may have moved by
now. Clearly, our, or strictly speaking, Bella's, plans had
changed.

During the previous week I had phoned a couple of
my contacts in the building trade to see if they could come
round at the weekend and give us a quote. The first duly
arrived at ten a.m. as arranged, measured up and showed
us some colour charts. The other contractor didn't show up
at all and Bella blamed me for this, which seemed a bit
unfair.

My prolonged absences during the week were now a
cause for concern to Bella and she made her frustrations
known.

"Who do you think does all the washing, the cleaning,
looking after the boys, preparing every meal, the ironing?"
At this point she picked out one of my shirts from the
laundry pile and said, "Well this is not mine", and then
another came out, "nor, is this," and she threw them in the
air. It caused Francis to vacate the room and he made a
tactical withdrawal to his bedroom as he'd seen all this

before. Sebastian, on the other hand, stood transfixed at the spectacle of his mother throwing laundry into the air in a fit of rage.

He shouted. "Stop, Mummy! Please stop mummy!" and started to cry.

At this point you are in a no-win situation. Well, what can you say or do? I did the only thing I thought sensible and tried to give her a hug but as I moved towards her, she pushed me away saying, "Leave me alone, go and look after your precious boys."

"Come on Sebastian, let's go and kick a football on the rec."

I called upstairs to Francis and I invited him too and the three of us retreated to the playground. I wondered how long we should stay out of the way until Bella calms down. The truth was, not long enough.

Once back inside an hour later, she moved closer to me and out of earshot from the boys said, "I hate you sometimes." It was said in a voice which was a cross between a threat and a hiss.

It seems shocking now to relate this story but at the time I was used to this behaviour, and I could always accept it without challenge or recrimination. It was just the way it was between us; however dysfunctional it may appear.

"What is the real problem, Bella?"

I never learn, do I? I had just lit the blue touch paper once more.

"Don't you start that again. You don't get it do you?"

This time, I made a tactical withdrawal to my study. I was once told that the man who understands women has not yet been born. I did try though to reason what I could have done differently or better to make her happy. Clearly, there was something within her that caused her unhappiness. As her husband, I hoped that she would confide in me more, tell me what fears and worries she bore, but sadly, her defences were secure and had been developed and tested over a long period of time, probably before we met, who knows.

Sunday, nothing was said, and we pretended all was back to normal. At bedtime she went through the same routine, and I lay quietly with my back to her as she turned the light out. A few minutes later and without any notice, she threw back the duvet covering me, rolled me onto my back and started sucking on my cock.

"Bella?"

"This is really what you want, isn't it?"

In honesty, yes it was. I tried to reach between her legs and play with her too, but she stopped me and moved further down the bed to avoid such contact. I tried to pull her back up the bed so I could lay on top of her, but she resisted that and said, "Just lay back", as her hand was moving up and down on me. She continued until I could not avoid the inevitable groaning.

We only went as far as Finsbury Park though.

***

In the morning I was driving back across the Pennines. I always liked the drive westwards in the morning as the sun, when it is shining, illuminates all that is in front of me, and the views were spectacular in that early morning light. It wasn't quite the same on a Friday driving the opposite way, as the sunlight was more from the Southwest and it seemed hazy. It was a tenuous link, however, I thought it seemed a suitable metaphor for my life.

I was trying to make sense of the weekend and I came to a startling conclusion. A logical and rational thinker like me will never understand an irrational woman like Bella. When I came to that summary, I stopped thinking about it for a while. It was odd though. Bella had shown no passion towards me last night, no kissing, no hugs, no intimacy, no sweet words. It was just sex. What was the difference between Bella and a prostitute?

***

For the next few weeks, I was able to keep Katie at arm's length. It was not that I didn't want to see her as she was great fun and a distraction from everything else, but it was going to make my life complicated even further. I popped round a few times just to catch up with news of the building project and we cuddled or what my dad would call 'heavy petting'. We certainly did not have intercourse and I did not stay the night. I feared making her pregnant, which was a peculiar thought as I didn't know if she was taking precautions or not. If I had enquired would that not give her the signal that I wanted to screw her?

Katie was really magnanimous once I was able to make her realise the complex situation I was in at home with Bella.

She agreed to give me the space I would need and she added. "I'm always here for you if you need me." What a sweet girl.

***

One thing a teacher or lecturer dreads is that moment when they are to be observed and assessed by their managers. I had notification from Mrs Ahmed that the professor will be observing my Structural Design 1 lecture next week. I was told that he may want to sit in for the whole lecture or part of it.

I made a point of rehearsing the lecture, something I never do, in my attic room one evening. I also had to provide a lesson plan outlining the salient points of the lecture, the aims and objectives and a summary of key points. Again, that is something I never normally do either. I was quite meticulous in my planning for this particular lecture and dutifully submitted my lesson plan to Mrs Ahmed on the Friday in readiness for Monday's lecture.

On Monday morning as the hundred plus students entered and settled down, I checked the TV monitors, the sound system, the camera, the documents I was going to refer to and for once all was in place. Phew.

Once I had started teaching the design of steel columns and showed the students how Euler's buckling theory is employed by using the slenderness ratio, I kept looking at the back of the theatre to see if Prof J-P was there. He wasn't but it didn't stop me glancing up every two or three minutes to see if he had crept in.

Halfway through the lecture, he was there in the back row making notes. At that point my mouth became terribly dry, and I found myself concentrating on teaching him alone, he was my only focus. Fortunately, I was able to give myself a stern talking to, kept my composure, relaxed, ignored him and looked intently into the middle ground.

At the end of the lecture, he came down the side steps while students were filing out.

"Come and see me this afternoon, dear boy, and we can have a de-brief."

"Yes, Professor."

"Very good," he said. "I enjoyed that." He had put my mind to rest until we met later.

***

Joanne looked up from her keyboard and said I could go in and see the professor now. There was no sign of Mrs Ahmed this afternoon.

I knocked on the door and pushed it open to be greeted by the cool air within this sanctuary. The professor was there, and Mrs Ahmed was sitting in the far corner preparing to take notes.

"Well done, this morning Phil," he said. "How was it for you?"

"Nerve racking," I admitted.

"No need. I liked your style of delivery, it was well paced and informative, covered the main points with some good examples. It was a bit difficult to hear at the back though."

I thought that the microphone should have sorted that out and I said so.

"Ah," he said. "Next time adjust the volume control beforehand and ask the students at the back if they can hear OK. Otherwise, excellent." He added, "Euler was a great mathematician, would you agree?"

"Yes." I wanted to say more to look a bit more informed. "Something of a polymath. I hadn't realised the influences he had on so many areas until I read a biography about him."

"Quite, so. The Germans had some great minds."

I avoided correcting him and saying that Euler was actually Swiss.

***

"Higher Uncle Phil," said Imogen, as I pushed her on the swing in the garden that evening. Jasmine waited patiently for her turn.

"My turn now," said Jasmine. Not so patiently then!

The girls alternated with monotonous regularity, but I didn't mind. It was lovely to hear their 'whoops' and 'whees'.

Anna appeared at the rear door and sang to the tune of London Bridge is burning down. "Dinner's ready, dinner's ready, come and get it, come and get it, right now, right now, if you want it,"

David was not back from work and Anna was close to dishing up food. She would need to plate his up separately again and pop it into the microwave for later. As it happened, David, came through the front door just in time to join us all for pasta and a cheesy sauce. Over dinner David asked the girls what they had been doing. I think he was asking them about what they had done at school. Jasmine acted as spokesperson.

"Uncle Phil played 'Uno' with us and then we played on the swing."

Anna could not restrain herself from saying, "Some men make time to play with their children when they get home."

David had a way of deflecting criticism without any drama. He smiled sweetly and said to the girls. "We can play 'Uno' later if you'd like or we can go round to the playground."

"Yes, please daddy. I want to go on the roundabout," said Imogen.

"I want to go on the rope slide," was Jasmine's wish.

"Me too," said Imogen, even though she knew she couldn't reach, and she was far too small anyway.

Fortunately, the girls were oblivious to Anna's comment, but I certainly wasn't and I'm sure David wasn't either. No doubt, he felt annoyed by the chastisement. For my part I felt awkward, it was as if I had inadvertently trampled over the family bond in size twelve boots. I thought it best to spend the evening in the attic on the pretext of working, but predominately, to keep clear.

***

It was coming towards the end of term yet again. I was always surprised how quickly it looms. This year, I was determined to get my final exam papers to the moderators in good time and I would avoid Greg's cheating and not regurgitate a past paper with different parameters. Also, I had to prepare the land surveying paper this year.

Timing in exams is critical. You can set whatever questions you deem appropriate, but each question needs to carry equal merit and sufficient time to complete. There is no point in setting a question that will take an hour to do when the rubric says they must answer four questions in two hours.

Question 3 on the surveying paper was going to be a theodolite traverse that would need a Bowditch correction. Once again, I set the bar much too high by having so many legs, combinations of acute, obtuse and reflex angles, co-ordinates, compass bearing from the origin. I timed myself in finding the correct solution and horrified to see it took me forty-four minutes, the students would need more time than that, even if they knew what to do immediately from the start. Oh dear, that will need scaling down. It was a similar thing on question 5 when I realised that the level survey, I proposed had far too many sightings (including negative sightings to the soffit of a fictitious bridge) and change points for it to be solved in just twenty-five to thirty minutes. I confess, in the end I did look at the past four years of papers to get a better understanding of the level (sorry, for the pun) that the questions should reach.

Nevertheless, I managed to get all papers ready for the end of term to be checked, moderated and sent to the printers. Additionally, I prepared the mark schemes as well to avoid any potential mistakes and/or missing information. It was quite embarrassing a few years earlier when I started teaching back at Lincoln to discover one of the questions in an exam could not be solved due to some missing data. I had to write on the whiteboard something like; 'Question 4. Please assume the depth of water in the reservoir to be twelve metres'.

**

As I had a free morning, I took the girls to school and had then agreed to take Anna to Irlam Locks on the old Manchester Ship Canal. It wasn't intended to be a sociable trip as Anna wanted to take photographs of the area and do some research on an old cold case murder back in the 1920's. A young eighteen-year-old boy was hanged for the rape and murder of a twenty-six-year-old woman who was travelling either along the canal or walking the towpath. The boy had always protested his innocence but there was so much circumstantial evidence against him that the jury felt obliged to convict and find him guilty. He was subsequently hanged in Manchester Prison.

Anna had done her historical research but wanted to walk along the area to get a real-life perspective. Even though the case was over a century old, she wanted to see if the jury were right to convict or whether this was a miscarriage of justice. She was certainly a good investigative journalist and writer. Being freelance, she was always struggling to find an outlet for her work and tried various newspapers, magazines, radio and TV companies. Her previous projects included the suffragette movement of the early twentieth century and identified the exploits and roles played by some extraordinarily brave women.

As we walked along the old tow path, I kept wondering if this was the first time, we had spent any time together on our own, without the girls or David. There had been times when we were in the house alone, but I don't think we had been anywhere else.

Most of our talk was fairly mundane and matter of fact but there were times when she let her frustrations out. She mentioned David's frequent times away from the house and the hours he spends putting his research together. She clearly admired him for what he was doing but the girls were missing out on his involvement with them, or rather, she thought he was missing out on them growing up.

Clearly, she was a bit sad that life was the way it was, but she had her work, friends and the choral group and that was all great. I wanted to give her a reassuring hug and hold her at one point but resisted the urge.

"You're a wonderful mother," I said at one point.

She turned her head quickly to look at me and smiled. "Thank you, You've been good to them too. They love you. Did you know that?"

"Oh, they'll love anyone who brings them treats and presents."

"No, it's not just that, they know you care for them."

It was true, I did. Of course, I loved Francis and Sebastian without any shred of doubt, however, Imogen and Jasmine were special too.

Later in the morning, we found a café by the water's edge, I bought us some toasted sandwiches and coffee and we sat outside in the sunshine. In that light she looked radiant and for a time, comfortable and relaxed. I thought she looked wonderful.

"How are you and Bella getting on at the moment?" she asked, quickly adding, "I'm sorry, I shouldn't have asked, that was rude of me."

Actually, I was relieved that she felt she could ask about Bella and me. If nothing else, it showed that Anna was comfortable enough with me to enter into a discussion of this nature.

"No, it's fine. I don't think a move to Manchester is going to happen anytime soon though. The boys are used to the situation, and I seem to be a peripheral figure somehow."

"You have a good relationship with the boys and that will not be broken. If I know anything about boys, they tend to be more resilient than girls."

When she said that, it made me wonder about her girls. "Are the girls all right?"

"Yes, they're fine but they don't see very much of David. He works long hours, weekends too. Even when he is at home, he is engrossed on the PC dealing with whatever statistics he is studying."

"I admire his tenacity. I am not sure I could maintain that level of commitment."

"He certainly is single minded that's for sure," then added, "determined might be better, I guess."

"He loves the girls though, surely?"

She was pensive for a moment and was careful to phrase her next comment so as not to appear disloyal.

"I'm not sure he ever really wanted children. I mean, he seemed happy when Jasmine was born."

"I have never regretted having Sebastian and Francis. Your whole life gets flipped over when your child is born." I tried to defend David. "Perhaps he is not good at showing emotion, that's not to say he doesn't love them."

"Perhaps you're right," she said, but not convincingly.

Our conversation came to an end when we noticed a Grey Heron flying just a few feet above the water and landing on the far side in its search for fish in the shallows. I wanted to talk more about how she felt. I wanted to say more about the dysfunctional relationship Bella, and I had fallen into. At that moment, it was not the right time, and it would all have to wait for another day.

***

Before the end of term, I felt I should see Katie and make sure she was all right before I was away for the next three weeks. I rang the bell but she didn't answer so I left her a note saying I would be away until next term and if she needed any help with the builders, to let me know. The note was a bit cold and matter of fact and I cursed myself for not saying more once it had dropped through her letter box.

Much later in the evening she phoned me and was clearly annoyed.

"Well, that wasn't a nice gesture, was it?" she started.

"Sorry?"

"Just leaving me a letter telling me 'You were off and see you next month'. It's not very kind or considerate, is it?"

"No, I'm sorry, please let me explain…" she wasn't going to let me explain.

"I thought we had something meaningful; I know all about Bella and am prepared to give you time to sort the situation out but you could have been more gracious, kinder, considerate, you didn't even leave an 'X' at the bottom!"

"Katie, listen, please." It went quiet for a moment.

"I'm listening," she said.

"I wasn't sure who would find the note. It may have been your parents or the builders that picked it up." Poor defence, I know.

"Why would anybody read a note addressed to 'Katie'?"

She was right, it was a bit thoughtless of me, so I apologised and arranged to see her now, even though at was half ten in the evening.

As soon as she opened the door, we were straight into a passionate clinch and kissed. I caressed her breasts outside her tank top and allowed my hands to grip her bottom, but I resisted the urge to strip her naked and I was keen to keep my clothes on.

Being face-to-face made it easier to explain the situation I was in, and she softened considerably. We talked idly about what might happen in the future. It was idle chat too because none of the scenarios appealed to me at this precise moment. She kept saying we wouldn't know if it worked between us unless we gave it a go, I countered that by pointing out that can't happen while I'm still with Bella.

Then she hit me with a bombshell. "Are you falling in love with Anna? Is that why you don't want to move in with me?"

My God, this woman was perceptive. I had to play a straight bat to this one.

"Of course not. Firstly, she is married to David, and they are very happy." First lie. "Secondly, I am still married to Bella, and she may still want to move here to be with me." Second lie. "Thirdly, I could not break up the girls' family." That one was true.

"I'm sorry," she said, "I am just a bit emotional that's all."

***

It was past midnight when I quietly let myself in and crept up to the attic.

I lay awake for a while thinking about what Katie had said. Was I still in love with Bella? Was she in love with me? I reasoned that the passionate part of our marriage, albeit low key, was over and had been replaced with mundane domesticity. I was unable to remember the last time we said, 'I love you' to each other. Had I fallen in love with Anna? It was a ridiculous scenario to contemplate really. Anna and David were together, perhaps not happily, but they had the two girls and their work. They appeared content with each other. I could not and would not wreck their marriage. Was I falling in love with Katie? I had to admit to myself that Katie had been good for me, really good. She listened to me with genuine concern and care. She was passionate, sexy and great fun but I did not have that chemistry or zing when we are together.

My mind twirled away like a windmill until I slipped into an uneasy sleep pattern.

Chapter 12

Easter should have been a good time back in Lincoln. Clearly the time with Francis and Sebastian was special. We celebrated their birthdays together this year by going ten pin bowling with several of Francis' friends and a couple of Sebastian's. We hired two alleys, one for the bigger boys (including me) and the other for the younger ones (including Bella). The little ones used those ramp frames to help direct their bowls and it was comical but touching to watch bowl after bowl slide inexorably into the gutters. Mind you, Francis and his friends didn't do much better. Dinner out, by a clear majority, was Pizza Express even though Sebastian wanted to go to McDonald's. We were able to appease him by saying the ice cream in Pizza Express was better than McDonald's.

Francis was now fifteen, taller than his mother and had started to shave. His voice had also broken, and I couldn't remember when it had changed. Acne and BO was also a curse that befell the poor boy and I tried, unsuccessfully, to help him manage both.

"Leave me alone, Dad." He would say.

I was also wondering about whether I should talk to him about sex and relationships. Bella laughed and said they'd already done that at school. That was a relief as my dad sat me down when I was fifteen and tried to tell me all about 'where babies come from'. It was the only time I saw him completely out of his depth. He started by asking if I knew what a girl looked like down there, pointing downwards. Then he talked about what happens to a boy, down there, when you see a girl, you really like. This was getting embarrassing for both of us. At this point his words dried up and he resorted to sign language by pointing his right index finger to a loop he made with his left index finger and thumb.

In sheer desperation, he said, "It's like a mortice and tenon joint, son." Then dad made some excuse to watch the news on the TV and left me very confused.

***

I was able to catch up with dad when I took the boys over to Boston one day. I did not remind him of the 'mortice and tenon' reference but I did ask how he managed to get me a job with a Consulting Engineer when I was sixteen. Sadly, he couldn't recall but thought he must have been talking to someone from their office when they visited one of his building sites.

One of the satisfying things was to watch Francis and his granddad together. Francis was now of an age when he appreciated the various things his granddad had done. Granddad could always tell some good stories from his days on the building sites and Francis was eager to hear them.

Sebastian had now turned eight and he and Francis had joined the colts cricket club at their respective age groups. The cricket club had erected nets on the recreation ground, as the boys were members, it was possible to go over during the day and use them. As a birthday present, we kitted out Sebastian with bat, pads, helmet and gloves and Francis got a better-quality bat. We left it to Francis to explain the need for a box to his younger brother.

Things had not improved between Bella and I sadly. There was a tension that hid below the surface of, what appeared to the public perception, to be a contented family group. I never pushed any buttons in the bedroom department for fear of letting off an explosion. Occasionally, I would send out a scouting party to see if an advance of the main troops may be welcomed but I was prepared for a hasty retreat. I was about to say, a withdrawal, but I didn't want that to be misconstrued. As I slid across the bed towards her with an erection, I used to think it could be considered as an assault with a friendly weapon. Her sense of humour did not match mine sadly, more often than not, the canon was not fired.

One evening we were watching TV and the telephone rang. Bella answered it.

"Hello?" and after a slight pause, Bella said, "It's for you," and handed me the receiver.

"Hello?"

"Hello" Katie said. "I'm sorry, I didn't intend to call but I just wanted to make sure you are OK."

"I'm fine, thanks." But I wasn't fine as my heart rate must have increased dramatically, I wondered what Bella would be thinking and what I was going to say.

"I know I shouldn't have called but I wanted to hear your voice. I've missed you and needed to make sure you are OK."

"That's fine." It was difficult to find the right words so as not to draw too much attention to myself or create any suspicion with Bella. Bella sat right beside me watching TV but had turned the volume down slightly. I continued to talk to Katie.

"Can I phone you tomorrow morning?" I knew Bella would be out then.

"Oh, yes, please, I'll be in anytime. So, so, sorry to have disturbed you."

"That's not a problem, really." I hung up and Bella wanted to know who that was. I didn't lie.

"It's that lady who wants a loft conversion. Do you remember I did all those drawings and specifications for her?"

"So why do you need to phone her back in the morning?"

Now I lied. "She wants me to talk to her builder about how the floor joists are to be supported."

***

In the morning I phoned Katie, and the phone only rang twice before she answered.

"I'm sorry, Phil. Will you forgive me for phoning you last night?"

I did of course but I had to make it clear to Katie that it was a very stressful situation. We talked for another hour or so and she had calmed down. I promised her that I would see her the week after next when term resumed. The builders still had not given her the quotes, but she was expecting them soon. Then we could talk about the next stage, which I took as a euphemism of either our relationship or the loft conversion.

***

Somehow, I got roped in to be a cricket umpire for Sebastian's little age group. I tried to be lenient with the number of wides and no-balls that were being delivered and gave the benefit of the doubt to the batters for lbw. Even eight and nine-year-olds can be quite vocal in appealing for a dismissal. When Sebastian came into bat wearing his oversized pads, wobbly helmet and gloves my heart skipped a beat. I gave him the guard in front of his stumps and waited with dread. The ball hurtled towards him, and he managed to hit it and set off for a run to the other end. The fielder fumbled the ball and so Sebastian made his ground safely. I was the most relieved person on the field.

It was lovely to see both my boys taking a keen interest in cricket and watching football. There was a real bond between the three of us and I wished that Bella could share this too.

When Bella was at work, Francis and I were in the nets and Sebastian was playing with Stevie, one of his friends, over at his house. I had bowled to Francis for nearly thirty minutes and my right shoulder started to complain.

"Let's have a break," I said.

He sat on the grass, and I sat on a nearby bench, and we drank from our respective bottles. We talked about the various shots he had played; when to come forward, when to go back in the crease, trigger movements to get his feet moving and so on. It seemed the right time to have a serious discussion, after all he only had one more year left at school before he started A levels.

"I think your mum will never be happy moving to Manchester now."

"She might Dad. When we leave school perhaps."

"That's going to be a very long time."

Francis corrected himself by saying that Sebastian will be leaving primary school when he himself finishes his A levels. Three years' time. It was a thought but not very palatable.

"Look, you know I'm staying with David and Anna, and it should have been a temporary solution. I feel as though I have overstayed my welcome. What would you say if I got myself a place of my own?"

"You mean you'll leave us?"

There was genuine panic and concern in his voice.

"No, not necessarily. I was thinking I could spend more time in Manchester. You two could come and visit me and stay over. You know, go to Old Trafford for the cricket, watch Man City, there's lots to do there."

"What about mum?"

"Well, I'm not thinking of getting a big place, just a small flat or studio apartment." I added unrealistically. "If your mum wants to come and stay that's fine, and I can come back here too."

It wasn't convincing.

"Are things that bad between you and mum?"

"Have you noticed?"

"You do argue a lot and it upsets Sebastian."

"Not you?"

"Yes, I suppose so, but it's been going on for a long time."

I had to admit it had. You can never fool kids; they know when things aren't right.

* * *

I was also able to catch up with John briefly. It was a chance encounter as he was at Tesco's petrol filling station at the same time as me. We decided to have a cup of coffee in the supermarket café for a quick catch up. He told me things hadn't changed much, Maria and he were still living in the same house but had their own bedrooms, two separate fridge freezers, allocated cupboards between them, agreed times that each would be in the kitchen. She had the lounge, and he had the spare room. She had the en-suite, and he had the bathroom. He also ignored the men she brought back and there seemed to be quite a number of different blokes. His feelings for her had now gone and they passed like ships in the night. John had started to see a new lady friend, Sandra, from Gainsborough.

"If you think parts of Lincoln are rough," he said, "you should see Gainsborough."

"Is Sandra good for you?"

He thought for a moment, looked up, smiled and nodded. "Yes, yes, I think she is."

"Is she a moaner?" I quickly added. "No, don't answer that question."

We laughed at that. I wasn't able to tell him my situation had changed because, basically, it hadn't.

***

Anna looked so fragile that first evening back in Manchester. It had been an unusually hot day for May, and she looked exhausted, and it appeared she may have been crying, although it could have been the heat. She was wearing a long white dress, but it could probably double as a housecoat. It was draped around her almost like a cotton sheet. She was barefoot and her long hair was held back with a scrunchie.

"Hi," I said.

Her voice was quiet, and she spoke softly and slowly. "Hello. Welcome back. I've done nothing about dinner, I'm sorry. I will get something sorted in a moment."

"Where are the munchkins?"

"Playing in the garden. They've already eaten, and I just didn't fancy anything."

"Look, let me go and say hello to the girls and I will get you a chicken wrap or something from down the road."

I went and saw the girls in the garden, Jasmine was reading a book in the shade and Imogen was playing with My Little Pony and a doll.

Jasmine said, "It's Uncle Phil," and they walked over and hugged me. It was so nice to know that they were so comfortable with me.

"Is your mum, OK?" I asked Jasmine.

"She's been crying." Kids can be so honest and forthright.

"OK, I'll go and see if I can cheer her up."

Back in the cool of the house I asked Anna what I could get her and David from the takeaway. Anna said that David wasn't here this week as he was in Helsinki at a conference. He left yesterday and wouldn't be back until next Saturday. I was going to say something inane like 'That must be so difficult for you' when I realised that Bella has this every week in term time. I excused myself from guilt and told myself that Bella didn't really care anyway. I wasn't sure that was true but when you are so far away, any crumbs of comfort will help.

"I'm sorry. Now you have to put up with me and I can see why that would be upsetting." I joked.

She laughed, but it was a reluctant one, more of a 'humph'.

We settled for cheese on toast and for once she let me help her in the kitchen.

I always hung back when it was time for the girl's bedtime. It didn't seem right to walk into their rooms or baths uninvited. They still had that beautiful innocence and naivety and long may that continue. Tonight, was different. Anna asked me to join her as we showered them in the bath with luke-warm water; they shrieked with delight, screwed up their eyes and shook their heads while jumping up and down and splashing in the bath. Afterwards we wrapped them in towels, dried them and put them to bed. Anna read to Jasmine, and I read to Imogen. Imogen fell asleep quickly and she only needed a sheet to cover her rather than the duvet.

I was the first downstairs, loaded the dishwasher with all the bowls, plates, cups and cutlery that had accumulated during the day.

When Anna eventually came down, she apologised for the mess and not getting food ready.

"I must be the worst mother in the world."

"I told you last term when we went to Irlam that you were a wonderful mother. Nothing has changed my mind."

"Thank you, Phil. Do you mind if I have an early night?"

I said of course not and with that she had gone. I pulled out a can of Heineken from the fridge, poured the contents into a glass, went into the garden and settled down to read 'The Calculus Wars' by Jason Bardi. I started to feel like this was my home and within minutes I was asleep myself.

***

Structural Design 2 filled me with dread at the beginning of the year. It was to be delivered by a series of lectures to the final year students and consisted of topics I had never designed myself while I was in industry. Clearly, I had designed such things when I was a student in Bristol but that was over twenty years ago. Now I was to show students how to design long span post tensioned concrete beams, the sort you may see daily spanning across motorways or railways. In the end it was a fairly painless exercise once you've selected the grade of concrete and required number and size of tendons, then make allowances for material safety factors, creep of the steel, shrinkage of the concrete and fatigue you are almost there. The only tricky bit is deciding the depth of the tendons to ensure a uniform stress distribution.

I felt particularly proud of that lecture.

***

I did go and see Katie that first week as promised and she had now got two of the three quotes she was expecting. The costs involved were more realistic, but she hadn't bargained for the VAT on top and that would definitely stretch the budget. Fortunately, her parents were prepared to pay for the bulk of the work, so it was likely to go ahead.

Of course, the conversation about the loft conversion came after the emotional reunion she hoped for. We kissed, caressed and stripped to the waist.

"Can we go to bed?" she said. "We don't have to do anything if you don't want but I just want to feel you close."

It was time for some honesty.

"Look Katie, you are a beautiful girl and I think you're great but you may want children one day and I won't want that, I have two adorable boys already. I am fifteen years older than you and I don't want us to get so deep that if coming out causes us real long-term pain I couldn't bear to hurt you like your ex."

"I know all that, I still want us to go to bed."

I told her about David's trip to Finland and that Anna was on her own and feeling weak. I will go back there this evening.

"I understand. You needn't worry, I'm on the pill. Take me to bed."

I wanted to show her I did care properly. Once in her bedroom, which was as small as the lounge, I slowly removed the rest of her garments and took off my clothes too. I started at her feet, along her shins, her thighs and then slowly pushed her legs apart to allow my tongue to dance around her clitoris, my fingers entered her vagina as gently as possible. After a few minutes her head jerked to one side, her back arched and her legs twitched uncontrollably. Her moan was so familiar but higher pitched. I shouldn't have these thoughts, but I couldn't help thinking, why was Bella never like this with me?

I lay beside her and cuddled her as she panted. In a breathless voice she said, "If this is the only time, we are to be together, I want to know what it's like to be with you, I want to feel you inside me, even if it never happens again, please, fuck me. Just fuck me."

***

It was almost midnight by the time I got back to the house and Anna and the girls were safely tucked away and in dreamland. I felt in dreamland too, Katie was true to her word, and she never made any further demands but that night we had been like a pair of animals for a few hours. She seemed insatiable but I was up for the challenge and there appeared to be no boundaries with her. There was one thing for sure, I was going to sleep well tonight.

***

I took Jasmine to Brownies on the Thursday evening and picked up a few things Anna needed from the mini mart. Opening the door, I froze momentarily as Anna's clear angelic singing came from the lounge. I just listened carefully to what she was singing, and I recognised it as 'Windmills of your mind'. I stood rooted in the hallway and waited for her to finish.

At the end, her little audience of one, Imogen, clapped and said, "That was lovely mummy."

I came through and said, "I couldn't agree more Imogen, your mummy has such a lovely voice."

"Oh, my God, I thought you were going to wait for Jasmine!" Anna shrieked.

"It's OK, I'll collect her in half an hour."

"God, this is so embarrassing," she said as she went to switch off the karaoke disc in the player as it started the next track 'Solsbury Hill'.

"Oh, I love Solsbury Hill," I said.

"OK, your turn then."

"Oh my God, now that would be truly embarrassing. I haven't sung properly for ages."

With that I made my excuses and prepared to head off to collect Jasmine.

***

When Jasmine and I came back, I opened the door and Imogen rushed to her big sister and whispered something in her ear. The two girls jumped with joy and said, "Yes, yes, Uncle Phil!"

"Sorry? What about Uncle Phil?"

Jasmine said, "You and mummy can sing together."

"What?"

Anna appeared at the end of the corridor with an expression which was a mixture of a grin combined with an elf like impishness.

"I will if you will," she said. "Our audience is assembled."

That just started the girls off again and they shrieked with joy and ran into the lounge in pure expectation.

"Anna, I can't, it's been too long, I won't know any of the words."

She thrust a piece of paper into my hand with the lyrics printed out.

"But I…"

"Come on," she said, "You mustn't disappoint your paying audience."

"What payment?"

"They've got ice cream for you afterwards. Come on."

So, we sang 'Islands in the Stream', but I was not good and I had to take the lead off Anna at times. I knew full well if I made eye contact with Anna, I would be an emotional wreck so I kept my eyes firmly looking at the lyrics. At the end the two girls clapped and cried for more.

"Oh, no. I'm done. For one night only…"

"Solsbury Hill?" Anna reminded me.

"Another time."

It was Jasmine that made sure that I promised. Anna looked wonderful tonight and I was so relieved that she had rallied from Monday. Much later in the evening after the girls had fallen asleep and while I was working upstairs I heard her singing again. This time she sang 'Yesterday once more' by The Carpenters, and I'll be honest, it was playing havoc with my emotions. As she sang the last verse, I had visions of Anna from all those concerts we sang back in Lincoln came flooding back and I remembered her so clearly singing so pure and serene. It was yesterday once more.

Chapter 13

"Why did you tell Francis that you're getting a place in Manchester?"

"I didn't say that, I said I was thinking about it because I couldn't stay at David and Anna's indefinitely."

"Well, talking to me first might have been nice."

"We have spoken about it."

"We had agreed not to talk to the boys until we were sorted."

I was not sure Bella was right about that, but it was easier to cave in now before this escalated any further. I apologised again and told Bella that it was a random chat I had in the cricket nets with Francis. Looking back at this time with Bella, I can only describe our relationship as a ship that has been holed below the waterline and no matter how hard the pumps are working it was still sinking. It's a poor metaphor but the only one I could come up with.

***

The following week I rang the bell and turned the key as usual to let myself in. David was back and he was in the kitchen with Anna and Imogen. Jasmine was upstairs reading.

"Hello David, welcome back, how was Finland?"

He told me about the conference, the weather, the flights and how clean he thought Helsinki was. Apparently, he was one of the guest speakers at the conference. I was suitably impressed. We opened a couple of cans of Heineken while Anna cooked dinner. I noticed that she was not contributing to the conversation, but she probably had heard it all before.

David also said, "I gather you and Anna have been singing together."

I replied. "Well, Anna was singing, and I was trying to keep in tune."

Anna interjected. "You were fine…"

"Do you fancy joining our choir sometime, Phil?" David interjected.

"I would like to get back to singing when we are settled properly."

Much of the evening followed similar evenings, the girls got ready for bed, Jasmine wanted me to read to her, I marked some scripts, David watched TV and Anna was writing notes following more of her investigations.

I turned into bed late, probably close to midnight but needed to visit my bathroom on the first floor. I always made a point of being as quiet as possible when walking on the floor as these old Victorian properties can have squeaky floorboards. In the past eighteen months that I had been staying, I could plot a route in the dark to avoid any of the creaks. Passing the door to David and Anna's room, there came from within the unmistakeable sound of love making. It was clear that the noise was coming from David as his grunts became more audible and the frequency increased. The iron bedstead started to join in this orchestration as it was gathering pace. The grunts and the squeaks from the bed were picking up the pace. Shortly after, the percussion section started as the head of the bed was beating against the wall and David was conducting this bizarre orchestra. I could not make out any sound coming from Anna but then I didn't want to hear that. It was all quite surreal, and I didn't want to be there, but I was frozen like a rabbit in headlights. My stomach knotted as I beat a hasty retreat along the well-known route back to the safety of my attic room. Lodging as I was in their house, it would be conceivable (sorry, let me re-phrase that), it would be perfectly possible that an embarrassing moment like that to occur at some stage. They were a happily married couple doing what happily married couples do, it's just that I wasn't expecting my reaction to be so gut wrenching.

***

In the morning I breakfasted early, left to go swimming and tried to block out what I had heard last night. I had a strange feeling in my chest, a sort of tightening which seemed to restrict my breathing and made me feel uncomfortable all day.

I had avoided visiting those girls on the street or in the little terrace houses with their red glows for some time. I told myself that it wasn't appropriate nor sensible to go there.

***

That next night was different as I still had that inner unease and genuinely felt lonely. I could have visited Katie, but I would not be able to tell her the truth, besides that would be using the girl and I did not want to do that.

"Are you looking for anyone special?" she said at the open window of the passenger door.

I invited her in, and she directed me to her well-used spot in this secluded car park within some office complex. We agreed to have straight sex but in a car, it is not easy. I would have to climb into the passenger seat well and kneel between her legs, she had already pushed the passenger seat as far back as it would go and had removed her knickers, pulling up what little skirt she wore. She played with me until I was hard enough to put on a condom, which again came apparently from nowhere. In my mind I had now separated sex with these girls from lovemaking and it was as mechanical for me now as it was for her, I imagined.

I took my time with her, pushed my middle finger into her vagina briefly and then entered her. It wasn't long before I gave out my familiar moan and it was all over. For a brief moment I stayed inside her and looked closely at her face, she was only a young woman, probably no more than eighteen or nineteen. Her perfume was quite strong and her brunette hair was long but tied back with a band. Her features were sharp as she had strong cheek bones, nose and forehead. She was not unattractive and in my youth I could imagine wanting to date such a girl.

Here I was, at forty-five years of age, a professional lecturer at an esteemed university, married with two young children shagging a girl who probably has just left school. I was old enough to be her father for Christ's sake. Had I slipped into some parallel universe where my morals had evaporated? Whichever way the moral compass was pointing, I was at this particular moment kneeling between the legs of this young girl with my cock deep inside her and half of me felt on top of the world, whereas the other half of me was in the pits of the earth. I didn't like myself at this moment, although relieved, relaxed and fulfilled I also felt massively guilty and seedy.

Later, I would reflect on the madness of this whole shady business. Using logic to explain my actions did not bring any sensible summaries. I determined I was a man with testosterone coursing through my body and the urge to have sex was so strong that I could be reckless and extreme, a prisoner of my own hormones. I reasoned that had Bella been more loving and less insecure about herself, there would be no need for me to search out these girls. Then, as I have said before, combining logic and emotion will never get any resolution.

Once again, despite the relief and relaxation I felt it was also combined with shame and remorse. On my return

I went straight to my self-imposed prison in the attic to think about what I had done. The scent of her vagina still clung to my finger, for a few brief moments I took in the intoxicating smell, and smiled to myself and then shook my head at the paradox of my arguments.

***

For the rest of that week, I couldn't bring myself to be around Anna or David. It just seemed as though things had inexorably altered and there was nothing, I could do to change the way I felt. Each time I saw David I couldn't help but imagine him on top of Anna, grunting away. Each time I saw Anna, well I didn't want to think about it. Of course, they were oblivious to the torment going on in my mind, why would they think anything else? I made excuses to Anna about not being able to come back earlier in the evenings on the pretext of putting together the mark schemes for the final exams (even though I had already done them). I knew that if I sat eating dinner with the family my mind would inevitably return to that fateful moment on the landing outside their bedroom door.

***

One evening after leaving the department, I took myself to a local pub several hundred yards away from the campus in the hope that there would be no students who may recognise me there. It wasn't a regular student bar though and most of the clientele were like me; middle aged, depressed and sad individuals. Some had given up and were well on the way to alcoholism, but most had kept their humour.

"Hello, mate," slurred the guy standing next to me at the bar.

"Hi, how is your day going?"

"All right, mate, all right, not bad." I could only imagine how many pints he had had before I showed up. "You?"

"Not great," I admitted.

"Well, you look well enough. We don't get many guys in suits in here. You a poofter?"

I laughed. "No, definitely not, that's probably why I'm not feeling great."

"Ha, ha, ha. Bloody women eh? Can't live with them, can't live without them."

I felt I didn't want to say too much to a complete stranger, so I changed tack.

"Do you fancy another?" Not a kind thing to offer drinks to a drunk. Fortunately, he declined the offer.

"No mate, no, I better get back to the missus. That's kind of you to offer though, very kind."

"What's the food like in here?" I ventured.

"All right if you like eating crap. There's a decent fish and chip shop on the corner though."

"Thanks for the advice."

"You're welcome." He got off the bar stool and turned to face me. He shook my hand warmly like an old friend and said, "Nice to meet you, son. I hope you sort things out with your woman." He was about to turn away and stagger to the door when he thought of something very important and conspiratorial, turned back and quietly said, "Let me give you some advice, son. Give her a good shagging, that will sort it out." He touched his nose, winked and was off.

I sat down at a table away from the bar with my pint and started to read one of the local rags, but my mind wasn't on that. I just used the newspaper as a guard against any other drunks offering me conspiratorial advice. 'Just give her a good shagging,' he had said. If only. It was time to give myself some good advice, but not there at that moment, instead I wanted to look and study the faces in the bar and wonder how their lives had been altered by the ravages of time and circumstance and mused about how their lives may have been shaped.

***

The time for thinking came on the way back to Lincoln on Friday afternoon. The weather wasn't great; overcast, drizzly over the hills but the traffic moved smoothly enough. To be honest, I hadn't really thought anything about my situation but an hour into the journey came the unmistakeable voice of Dusty Springfield singing 'Windmills of your mind'. It was like an electric shock. I turned up the volume and imagined Anna singing it. Of course, the track finished far too quickly, I turned off the radio so as to keep the music swirling in my head and not be overwritten by whatever song the radio station was about to play next.

So here it is, I thought. Sort it out, once and for all.

Firstly, I have a wife who doesn't really love me. She may care for me, but she doesn't love me for myself. I have two boys who are getting used to me not being there and get anxious when Bella and I are together as they sense the tensions between us.

Secondly, I have the possible love of a sweet Jamaican girl. She is too young for me but she's great in bed. In time, she'll want to be with someone who will give her kids and can satisfy her.

Thirdly, I am working in a place I love and doing a job I've always dreamed of. I could give it up and go back to Lincoln, find another job and try and make it work with Bella. Or I could get a place of my own in Manchester, rent a flat perhaps. Or I could divorce Bella and use my share of the equity to buy a flat or house in Manchester. That way I could start dating again and find someone new.

Fourthly. There wasn't a fourthly really. I admitted to myself that I had fallen in love with Anna. She was happily married to David with two beautiful little girls and there was no way I could ever say anything to her. Besides I don't know how she feels about me. I am just the lodger, and it is convenient to have me around to babysit, run little errands, fill in the voids when David was at work.

The lyrics of 'Windmills of your Mind' seemed apt, and were forever spinning in my mind.

I am an engineer. Once again, how can logic ever overcome emotion?

***

"Tea?" Bella said as I came in the door. She had stopped even coming to the door to see me home, not even a perfunctory kiss on the cheek. There was a time we might have fallen into bed on my return from a week away fifteen or so years ago.

"Any post?" I asked.

"On the dining table." She called back from the kitchen.

I scanned the normal load of junk mail and there was nothing important again.

"Where are the boys?" I called back.

"Francis is playing cricket at Branston and Sebastian is playing at Stevie's." She again called back from the kitchen.

"Let's have a fuck then," I said in a lower voice.

"Sorry?" she said walking through with the tea. "What was that?"

"Fancy our luck then. Look, we've won a holiday in Bermuda," I said waving a piece of junk mail.

"That's just another con," she said.

"Yes, you're probably right," but the play on words was lost on her. It did make me smile though.

***

216

"Good morning, Marshall and Skinner," said the voice on the phone. It seemed a bit too bright and cheerful for a Monday morning.

"Morning. My name is Phil Avery and I saw that you're the agents for a flat on Princess Drive."

"Do you mind holding?" I was about to say that's fine but found that she'd already put me on hold anyway. After a few moments. "Yes, that's right, number 53 Princess Drive. Would you like to view the property?"

"Yes, please."

"We can have an agent there this afternoon."

"It will need to be late afternoon as I am teaching until four."

"Four-thirty?"

"Can we make it five?"

"Yes, you'll be met by Archie Davenport."

"Thank you," and I hung up.

***

It was a nice flat actually, a bit rough but fundamentally sound. It still had residents in-situ, but they were moving out in two months' time as they had already given the requisite three months' notice. It was on the second floor but there was a lock up shed for bike storage in a block close to the flats, no garage but plenty of parking spaces and a good view over a green and plenty of mature trees obscuring the view of the main road. I would be expected to provide my own white goods; fridge, freezer, washing machine and so on but the flat would be partly furnished with beds, settee, dining table and chairs, etc. That would be fine, I could make it mine, personalise it perhaps, probably not with beer mats on the wall or posters of 'Yes' and 'Genesis', but it could be good.

Archie Davenport was a typical Estate Agent, smarmy and smooth, well dressed and probably gay. But what the hell, he was only doing his job.

"Can I give you a decision tomorrow, Archie?"

"Of course, let me give you my business card and you can ring my mobile anytime, day or night."

Yes, he was gay.

I accepted the flat and the two-month lead in time would be perfect. I should get the keys during the last full week of term. The flat was about the same distance from the university as David and Anna's place but more to the north-east rather than the south and in my mind, I equated that to be equivalent to the vertices of an equilateral triangle. That way I could visit the girls occasionally, still babysit, perhaps, have meals with them still, see Katie and have Katie come and stay. The possibilities seemed endless.

***

The next week I had managed to get my emotions under control again. I got back to Anna's about six p.m. and dinner wasn't ready yet, so I gave the girls another swing and they were very good at taking turns. David still was not back from work, and I hoped he would not be back for a while yet. I still had that barbed comment in my mind when Anna had said to David, 'Look, some men play with the children after work' and I think David was probably as peeved as I was embarrassed.

The four of us sat around the table and Anna had made a risotto style dish that was actually very refreshing and tasty.

"Wow, this is good," I said, "Do you like it girls?"

They said they did, well Jasmine said 'yes' but Imogen just nodded and kept tucking in. The proof of the pudding is in the eating, isn't it?

"It was a simple recipe really," said Anna but I think she was pleased I made the effort to compliment her.

The girls were telling us about their day. Imogen said her friend Lucy fell over outside the childminders and cut her knee and needed to go to hospital.

"Blood everywhere," she announced with glee.

"Poor girl," said Anna. "What happened?"

Imogen explained she was running and tripped over a step in the path and fell over. She went to hospital. It did not require stitches apparently, but they put, "something sticky over it," was Imogen's best description.

Jasmine's news was more mundane, but she was keen for me to help her with some maths problems this evening.

"That's what your resident engineer is here for."

"So, pleased you are here," Anna said. "I'm hopeless with maths."

"I'm sure David is just as good with maths."

"When he's here," was her reply.

David didn't come in until nearly nine p.m. The girls had gone to bed and were now fast asleep and I was working in my attic room. I came down in order to be sociable and make a cup of coffee. Anna was nowhere to be seen, and I presumed she must have gone to read in bed or had fallen asleep in one of the girl's rooms. David took the risotto out of the microwave.

"What's this supposed to be?", he asked.

"Anna made a risotto."

I was about to say how tasty it was but before I could say anything, he said, "Good job I've eaten already then." He covered the food with another upturned plate and popped it into the fridge. "Fancy a beer?"

I was going to make a coffee, but beer was fine. We shared a couple of chilled cans of Heineken, and he filled me in on what he was doing at work and how one of his projects should be finishing this Friday although an extensive trial starts next week. It would take him all over the country to co-ordinate apparently. It was nice to talk but at no point did he ask how my job was going. Not that I could say much anyway.

I kept the news of the flat rental to myself for the time being.

***

The builders had started at Katie's, and she was keen for me to look at what they had done. She wanted me to keep an eye on things as she had no idea of the processes involved. In effect she wanted me to project manage but that was inappropriate for a small works contract. I did say that I would check everything as it went along. To be fair to the builders, they had started well.

"It's going to be a stressful time, Katie, they'll be loads of dust, mess, noise, you can forget about having a nice lawn at the front for a few months."

"You did warn me," she said.

We were comfortable with each other, and I half expected to go to bed with her. In the end we sat on the sofa, talked about our week, drank a huge cafetière of coffee with some mint chocolates that I brought round, and well, just talked. I wasn't sure how she may react to me getting a flat, it could have gone either way. On the one hand I might have been saying to her, 'I am not moving in with you' or on the other hand 'you are welcome to come and stay in my flat'. Best not to provoke a discussion on the matter.

We did have a passionate kiss before I left, and we caressed each other but I think we both realised tonight was not going to be a repeat of what happened last time.

***

As I walked back to Anna's I couldn't decide whether I was either relieved or disappointed at not going to bed with

Katie again. The way I felt, I would not have disappointed her now that I know which buttons to press to turn her on, plus, my little brain was saying, 'go on, go back and fuck her'. Naughty little brain.

***

A lot of my colleagues hate invigilation and with good reason. You sat there, for the most part, looking from the stage at the heads of students massed in the Hall feverishly writing away, picking up calculators, referring to charts and diagrams in an attempt to cram in as much as they can remember in the two hours. You are doing nothing.

I made a point of walking the course from time to time. Slowly moving down between the aisles turning at the bottom and then moving up the adjacent aisle, a bit like a combine harvester reaping the corn, except I was reaping nothing as my hands were firmly behind my back. Sometimes something exciting might happen, when a student had dropped a pen or pencil for example and I retrieved it for them, they would whisper, 'thank you' almost inaudibly; or handing out new pieces of paper as their allocation was being depleted. I looked forward to the time when I could announce, 'You have thirty minutes remaining' and for good measure, repeat 'thirty minutes remaining'. It was like a railway station announcer, 'the train on platform three is the 3:45 to Oldham', pause, 'the 3:45 to Oldham'.

As you can probably tell, I quite liked invigilation, it was a time for peace and calm, well at least for me. During the fluid mechanics exam it was just Simon and I invigilating. He was at the back of the Hall as I was doing my combine harvester routine. I had just got to the front of one of the aisles and turned to head back towards Simon when I spotted, he was doing a music hall routine, dancing sideways, clicking his heels and pretending to have a hat and cane. Keeping a straight face at that moment required me to have a very strong will. I love Simon.

***

We were getting close to the end of another academic year, and I wanted to take the family out for dinner as I did last year to Carlo's, you know, to say, 'thank you'.

"When would be a good day for me to take you all out to dinner? Like we did last year, but we can go somewhere different this time."

Anna said the girls would love that and we agreed that Thursday was a good day as Brownies had finished for the summer. We gave the girls the choice of where we went, and I hoped that it would not be a split decision between Pizza Express and McDonald's like Francis and Sebastian's birthdays.

"Carlo's, Carlo's, Carlo's," they sang in unison. So that's settled then, a week on Thursday.

***

It had been a few weeks since Anna coerced me into singing with her and fortunately no more was said and I thought the girls had forgotten. After all, our evenings were never constant.

"Uncle Phil?" Jasmine started. "You promised to sing to us."

"Yes, yes," echoed Imogen.

Anna raised her eyebrows and smiled. "Well?"

"Oh no, do I have to? I have a terrible singing voice."

The three of them disagreed with me and Anna said, "I wouldn't suggest it if I thought you couldn't sing."

So, the cat was out of the bag, Anna had reminded them. It was a good job David wasn't there because there was absolutely no way on earth, I would have done it.

"All right, all right, but on one condition. Mummy sings a song, and then me and then we both sing together."

"That was not the deal," Anna said.

"OK. We don't do it then."

The audience were not having that. "Come on, mummy."

Anna reluctantly got out the karaoke disc and set it up. I had thought this moment might happen and I did try and prepare by practising in the car to and from Lincoln.

Anna sang, at my request, 'Yesterday once more' and it was just as I imagined her all those weeks ago when her angelic voice floated up to the attic.

The girls were in raptures.

Now, it was my turn and to keep the mood I sang 'The sound of silence' by Simon and Garfunkel. The first time I sang this was, strangely enough, in Lincoln Cathedral when I was a kid, and our junior members of the choir were asked to give a recital at a music festival.

The girls were so enthralled as these two people they knew so well had serenaded them.

"Now mummy and Uncle Phil," prompted Jasmine.

We sang 'Islands in the stream' again and this time I nailed it. I was also able to keep eye contact with her and she was the only person in the world at that moment.

At the end the girls were clapping and giggling as hard as they could.

I gave Anna a hug.

It was the first time, surprisingly, we had actually made such close physical contact and there was no mistaking the chemistry between us, and she couldn't hide her feelings either. We moved away from the hug, but we kept holding hands looking into each other's eyes. Her wide eyes said it all. Her expression was serious, and she was biting her lower lip. The girls were still applauding, oblivious to the realisations that had befallen their mum and me. I resisted the strong urge to lean forward to kiss her. I am sure she detected the look in my eyes.

Now I knew how she felt, and I knew I had to leave and never come back.

Chapter 14

Bella was in the front garden when I pulled onto the drive.

"You're back a bit earlier than normal."

"Well, it's exam season again and I thought I would mark the papers here."

"Tea?"

"Yes please."

At some point this weekend I am going to have to say I have a flat in Manchester lined up. I am due to pick up the keys in a fortnight and I couldn't put it off any longer. On the way back home, I kept playing out all those scenarios again and again.

Scenario 1. Leave Manchester, get a job back here, try and make it work with Bella.

Scenario 2. Take the flat, have the boys there for weekends and holidays, separate from Bella, start again with someone new.

Next week I will spend as little time with Anna as possible, apart from taking them to Carlo's and I will say, as kindly as possible, I have found somewhere else to live. I will promise to come and see them, but I will, of course, break my promise. It is time to move on. But in which direction?

"Hi John, how are you?"

His voice was a bit distant on the phone. "Fine. You?"

"Do you fancy meeting up later this evening?"

"Sorry, no can do. I'm off to Gainsborough this evening."

"Tomorrow?"

"I can do lunchtime. How about 'The Kings Head' at twelve?"

"Great, see you there."

***

That evening we sat round the dining table eating almost in complete silence. It didn't seem natural, and I knew that if the girls were here, they would be chatting away nineteen to the dozen.

"How are you finding school Francis?"

"OK."

"Would you like any help with maths or science?"

"No, not really."

"How about you Sebastian?"

"What about?"

"Would you like any help with schoolwork?"

"Not really."

Bella never talked about her work at the law firm, citing confidentiality, and she was never really interested in my work either when I was in the construction industry or now in academia. It didn't really give much scope for conversation.

"How are your mum and dad," I asked Bella.

"Just the same really. Dad has an appointment at the hospital next week."

I started to wonder what was on TV.

***

Meeting John at the Kings Head was an opportunity to have a proper chat, but I was to be disappointed.

"Can't stop long," John said, "meeting Sandra later."

"Is that going well?"

"Yes, she's a great girl. So different from Maria."

I had already got two pints of 'Poacher's' set up before he got there.

"Cheers," he said drinking about half of it in one go.

"Cheers."

"So, what's your news?" asked John.

"I'm getting a place in Manchester on my own."

"Bloody hell. What does Bella think of that?"

"She doesn't know yet."

"Fucking hell, good luck with that mate."

As we talked it was obvious John hadn't realised how bad things were between Bella and me. He kept saying 'Fucking hell, I can't believe it' when I told him about the (lack of) sex, the throwing of my laundry and how she said she hated me at times.

I did not mention Katie or Anna. I just said it was time for a fresh start, like him and Sandra perhaps. I knew John would keep in touch whatever. I was grateful for that as he has been a good friend for such a very long time.

"Well, I'm on the end of the phone if you ever need me," were his parting words.

***

Sunday evening was never a good time for discussions with Bella, but I could not put this off any longer.

"I'm thinking of renting a flat in Manchester for next year," was my opening gambit.

"Why would you need to do that? David and Anna said you can stay with them indefinitely."

"Well, I don't think they meant it to be this long."

"Have they said something to you then?"

"No, not really but the girls are getting bigger, and I am feeling as though I am in their way a lot of the time."

"It seems like a lot of wasted money renting somewhere when David and Anna let you lodge with them. Have you fallen out with them?"

"No, it's just that I need more of my own space while I am there."

There was a silence for a few moments and then she said, "Have you met someone else?"

"No, of course not, I'm at David and Anna's place every night. Anyway, why would I want to do that?"

That seemed to placate her, well, for the time being.

I was an old hand at this now. Exam papers marked, projects collated, spreadsheets prepared with grades and recommendations. Everything ready for the examination board on Friday afternoon.

There were two new pieces of information I received during that last week.

Firstly, I had been approached by the course director to ask me if I would be prepared to be a tutor for about twenty-five new students next year. That would be about a quarter of the intake. It was one aspect of my job back in Lincoln that I really enjoyed because you could really engage with the students, help them through the difficult times and see them grow and mature. Of course, I jumped at the chance.

Secondly, I was asked if I would like to join the research team in looking at the structural design implications in earthquake regions. Of course, I jumped at the chance as well.

It really felt as though I had become an integral member of the department. I even discovered Mrs Ahmed's name; it was Indira.

***

David had phoned Anna on the Thursday afternoon to say he might not be able to get back in time to go to Carlo's with us, but if he could get away in time, he would join us at the restaurant. As the four of us walked along the pavement to Carlo's it wasn't wide enough for us all so Anna held hands with Imogen and I walked behind holding hands with Jasmine. I had a heavy heart and was rehearsing my talk with Anna about the flat and how best to soften the blow.

Once we were inside 'Carlo's', I said to the waiter. "Hi. I have a table for five booked under the name of Avery?"

I couldn't remember if it was the same waiter who showed Katie and I to the cubicle or not, but anyway he led us to a nice bright and airy table.

"Sorry, there's only four of us at the moment but we may well be joined by another person later."

I thought I should be braver and order something different. Anna ordered an Italian seafood salad, and the girls were going to share a Margherita pizza.

"Lasagne, please," I said.

I could not find the right words to use to explain that I had agreed to take the flat and that next year I would not be coming back. I didn't want to spoil their evening as the girls were so happy and Anna looked wonderful. The stress and tiredness seemed to have evaporated from her and she looked serene. She wore sandals with a long cream dress and a burgundy tied belt, no, more of a sash. The girls wore matching party dresses. Being boring I was in my suit, but I had at least removed the tie.

Jasmine was keen on having a Neapolitan ice cream and Imogen wasn't going to pass over on that offer. In the end they had a knickerbocker ice cream with all the trimmings, nuts, chocolate sauce and wafer. The top of the fluted glass sitting in front of Imogen was taller than her as she sat at the table. It was such an endearing sight to watch her negotiate her long spoon into the glass to retrieve bits of ice cream. I am going to miss these little darlings next year.

We had finished by seven p.m. and David hadn't joined us, so we walked back home again but this time we switched partners.

***

Once we were back in the house, it was obvious that David had not returned as yet, and the girls were about to head upstairs to bed.

"Thank you, Uncle Phil," said Jasmine.

Her little sister just said, "Thank you," as they both disappeared upwards with Anna. I poured myself a Heineken from the fridge and went outside and sat in the warm evening air. I was making a complete mess of this.

Half an hour later, Anna joined me in the garden with a glass of wine.

"So, what has been bugging you all evening?" she said.

"Sorry?"

"There's something. I can tell."

Perhaps now we were close enough to read each other's mind.

"Anna... I'm going... no, I have, er... got a flat for next year." I looked down at the path while I stumbled over these words. I couldn't make eye contact with her. I just couldn't.

"Oh," there was a long pause. "Why? You know you are always welcome here. The girls will miss you dreadfully, they always ask after you."

"I shall miss them too. I will come and see them regularly. Still do all the same things."

"You don't mean that, do you? You won't see them again, will you?"

Without another word she got up and walked back into the kitchen and started finding jobs. Clearing away crockery into the dishwasher with more force than necessary and putting things in the cupboards with a purpose.

How could I tell her I loved her so much that it hurts being here?

I was about to go into the kitchen to see if I could tell Anna the real reason when David walked into the garden.

"I am sorry," he said apologetically. "Phil, we were so busy today and I am sorry to have missed Carlo's. Did you all have a good time?"

"Yes, it was good. I am sorry you were not able to be there too." As I said it, I realised I did not really mean it.

We went back into the kitchen and David continued talking about his work and why he was unable to get away in time. I kept looking over to Anna as I needed her to understand my motives, but she had her back to me while finding things to do in the cupboards, shelves, on the table or in the fridge. She did anything to avoid eye contact with me as she was clearly upset by my news. Under the circumstances, it would be best to remove myself from their vicinity, after all, had I not caused too much sadness this evening?

Without looking at me, Anna said to David that I was leaving tomorrow and probably would not be back next year. He was quite surprised at the news and started asking me what my plans were for next year. As I told David about the flat I was painfully aware that Anna had slipped away leaving us to talk. My last memory of her was the back of her cream dress and her long strawberry blond hair entering the shadows of the hall as she went upstairs to her bedroom. My heart sank but I tried to keep my composure as David was still deep in conversation about my future arrangements.

***

In the morning I rose early, well in truth, I had not slept much and was wide awake at five, tidied the room, piled up pillowcases and duvet, skipped breakfast, left the key on the table and a note that wanted to say more.

To David, Anna and the munchkins,

Thank you for everything you've done for me over the past two years. You have made me so welcome that I felt like another member of the family. I shall miss you all. Have a wonderful summer. Much love.

(Uncle) Phil xxx

Closing the door for the last time as quietly as possible, I walked along those familiar paving slabs and looked back at the stained glass in the transom window. I opened the boot of the car and placed my luggage inside. I looked back at the door in the hope that Anna would be standing there, but those things only happen in films. I drove to the swimming baths, changed and stood on the side of the pool. At that moment, it felt like another appropriate metaphor for my life presently, I had to take a deep breath, gather myself, dive in and continue to kick on regardless. There was no going back.

Chapter 15

Despite the fact that term had finished, I went back to Manchester on the Wednesday of the week after. I was on the way to Marshall and Skinners, Estate Agents to pick up the keys for Princess Drive and had arranged to collect them at noon.

As I approached the city, I had a strong urge to drive to Anna's. I wanted to know if she was all right as she had not contacted me since I left the note, but then again, why would she? I had abandoned her and the family.

I did the next best thing, I phoned Katie.

"Hi, Katie, it's me." We knew each other well enough for her to know 'it's me' meant 'Phil'.

We both wanted to know how the other one was, I told her I was in Manchester and wanted to see how the builders were getting on. She invited me to come and see but it would have to be this afternoon as she was out and about. That gave me time to collect the keys, drop a few things off at Princess Drive and get familiar with the flat first.

The girl at Marshall and Skinners had that bouncy voice I remembered.

"Hello, welcome, how can I help you?" she sang.

"I'm Phil Avery, I've come to collect the keys for fifty-three Princess Drive."

"Hang on a moment," and without waiting for me to affirm that I would, she walked into the back office. She came out with a document file containing all the legal paraphernalia that goes with rental properties; lease agreement, emergency procedures, telephone contacts, inventory, security arrangements, keys and duplicates, keys for windows and services cupboards, instruction manuals for extract fans, fire alarms, smoke and carbon monoxide monitors, etc. I started to think life was too short. Then there was the direct debit arrangements and deposit (which I had already given a couple of months ago, but that paperwork needed to be found). I signed this and that and eventually got out of there nearer one p.m.

Opening the door of the flat I was hit by an odour I hadn't detected before. It was the stale air of a secure space that had been left vacant for three weeks. I opened the windows as wide as possible and brought in the few bare essentials I had collected from the various items Bella was happy to discard; old kettle, mugs, a few items of cutlery and crockery together with tea bags, coffee, and I hate to say it, powdered milk. I needed to order some white goods very soon and have a fridge at least.

***

By the time I got there, the builders had left for the day and Katie opened the door. We hugged and kissed, but not the

237

passionate kiss we had experienced a few months earlier. Our relationship seemed to have cooled and plateaued onto a more platonic level.

"It's good to see you," she said with genuine care.

"You are looking good."

We talked about the end of term, life back at Lincoln, how the boys were doing, and of course, the building work. She gave me a tour, which didn't take long because she couldn't, or rather, didn't like climbing a ladder. I did go into the loft and was impressed at the work; it was clean and well-constructed. The dormers were in, the box beam purlins fabricated, and the existing struts and ties removed so there was now a clear space. The floor joists had been inserted but not the floor itself, so I had to tread carefully.

"They've made a really good job of it." I was able to put her mind at rest. "Once the floor and stairs go in, there'll only be the insulation, plasterboard and second fix carpentry and electricals. Then it will be ready for decoration."

Katie looked forward to decorating herself. Over a cold drink I told her about the flat and she took the news very well.

"I will be able to come and visit," she enthused.

"You'll be very welcome, and I would like you to see it at some stage. Once I've moved in, you'll be the first."

"Let me know when there's a bed," she said laughing.

I wasn't sure how to take that comment and so I did not pursue it. She had a mischievous side to her. In many respects I was happier with the way we were with each other now but part of me still wanted her.

"I am going to have to go soon. It's a long drive back to Lincoln."

"Oh, I thought you may have stayed with David and Anna to break up your journey."

"No, I didn't think of that," I lied and then continued because I needed to know. "Have you seen David or Anna recently?"

"No, I haven't." And that left me feeling rather down.

***

Back in Lincoln a couple of weeks later I had another example of why securing the flat may not have been such a bad move. Once again, it always started quietly and innocuously then built up to a crescendo. Bella's frustrations came to the surface, and I was the obvious target. At the time I would get very stressed by these episodes but in my lighter moments I would describe them as Led Zeppelin's 'Stairway to Heaven' but I renamed it 'Stairway to Hades'.

Simple little guitar riff. Easy lyrics.

"What are you doing today?" she asked.

"I don't know, I haven't made any plans. I could take the boys out if you like."

"Why? So, I have the house on my own?"

"Would you like time on your own?"

"Not really, but then it's convenient, isn't it? For you, I mean."

"Convenient?" I was getting confused.

Lead guitar joins in.

"Yes, so you can go out and have a nice time and I can clean the house, do all the washing, ironing, cooking, washing up and all the other jobs around the place."

"Well, what would you like to do Bella?"

"I haven't a choice have I, all these jobs need doing."

"Then I can help, what can I do?" said as calmly as possible.

"You don't notice these things, do you? Little wifey goes round doing all the chores and you three just sit around watching TV or playing games."

"We don't mean to make any mess." Calmer still.

"Don't you put that 'Mr Nice Guy' voice on as though butter wouldn't melt in your mouth."

Drums enter now.

"Look, Bella, I am not sure what you expect me to say."

At this point I stood up and moved towards her and put my arms around her. She saw it coming and as I tried to give her a cuddle, she immediately went on the offensive, pushing me away and shaking her head from side to side with her eyes closed.

Robert Plant was now in full cry and demonic.

"I hate you sometimes. Why don't you go back to Manchester? That's what you really want."

So, what do you do? The only sensible thing.

"Come on boys, footie?"

There's a lady we all know and she she's buying a Stairway to Hades.

**

"How do you fancy a trip to Manchester to see the flat, Francis?"

"Can we watch the Test Match at Old Trafford?"

"I can't see why not. Who's touring this year?"

"Pakistan."

This could work. I had told the family that I was going back to Manchester to receive all the things I needed there. I had bought a fridge/freezer and washing machine new, but I intended to get some other bits and pieces of furniture from second hand merchants.

"The place needs livening up a bit. Would you like to help?"

Francis said he would. Well, what he actually said was, "Yeah, whatever."

I set about checking dates for the Test Match and managed to secure tickets for day 2, which was on a Friday. I arranged delivery of the white goods for the Wednesday before but not until the afternoon and that would give us time on the Thursday to take in a few sights of Manchester and get some other bits and pieces. Whatever we needed we'd go out and buy, including dinner. It would be good to bond more with Francis as we hadn't done an awful lot of father/son things recently.

I was surprised that Bella agreed to let Francis come with me to Manchester but his arguments were secure and reasonable. He countered every objection she made with a solid and reasoned statement of his own. 'I can go and watch England play cricket at Old Trafford', 'I'm a big boy now, I'm fifteen for goodness sake', 'dad needs help sorting things out and he can't do that on his own', 'I can see Dad's office and work', 'It'll be a bit of a holiday'. My boy, I was so proud of him.

"Oh, for God's sake go then." The white flag was still waved with venom though.

The car was packed and everything we needed, or at least, thought we needed was safely in the boot.

"Come on Francis, we need to be there before the delivery guys get there."

"Coming Dad," I let Francis choose the music on the radio, but his head was buried in his iPad playing some game which I couldn't relate to, even after he explained what he had to do to get up each level. There are times I am grateful to be the age I am and not growing up in this bloody minefield of teenage angst.

Eventually we nosed into Princess Drive, and I could see Francis was not impressed.

"It's a bit run down Dad."

"It's only temporary, son. It's good for you to see for yourself what life is like for other folks."

I'm not sure he appreciated my philanthropic views, but his response was typical.

"Yeah, I suppose so."

When we opened the door to the flat his mood didn't lift either.

"It's a dump Dad."

"We can make it how we want it. Come on, live dangerously for once."

He smiled at the thought and went on a tour of the other rooms. It didn't take long; two bedrooms, a bathroom, the lounge/diner and a kitchen all accessed from the hallway in which we had entered.

The delivery guys hadn't let us down, but they were very late. It was six p.m. before they turned up, by six-thirty p.m. the fridge/freezer and washing machine were in place and working. Francis was hungry so I knew where to take him.

"Pizza Express?"

"Yes, great, is it far?"

"Come on." And we left the flat.

In the few hours we were there we at least managed to get the beds sorted, the towels, toothbrushes and toiletries in place. Breakfast cereals in the cupboard, milk and orange juice in the fridge. It was habitable and it was, for these three nights only, ours.

He was reluctant to do so, but I persuaded Francis to ring home and talk to Bella and Sebastian. He wasn't on the phone for long but at least he made contact. I didn't want to eaves drop but in a tiny flat there was not much choice. He told Bella he didn't like the flat when he first saw it, but he was enjoying himself now, been to Pizza Express, talked of our plans for tomorrow and how he was looking forward to the cricket. He sounded really upbeat and happy.

I knew Bella would be disappointed to hear this. She would have hoped that this little jaunt would be a complete and utter disaster.

Francis really opened up during those brief days away. We had so many conversations that never had materialised at home. We talked about his future plans, what A levels he may take, where they might lead him, what career path, medicine perhaps, what university he may go to if he gets the grades (I resisted the chance to say 'Manchester?' as that would be unfair), cricket, football, and yes, girls. I hadn't known that he had been 'going out' with Tracey from school for the past three months. I made the point of listening and only gave advice when he asked for it. I certainly didn't want to recreate the 'mortice and tenon' episode that my father negotiated with me.

***

On the Thursday morning we went out and bought some bits and pieces for the flat and I gave him a tour round the Etihad stadium as well as United's ground. We then went over to an almost deserted engineering department so I could show him my staff room, the lecture rooms and theatres (praying that those technicians were not in the AV room, fortunately it was all in darkness) and introduced him to Mrs Ahmed and Joanne in the secretarial office. His only comment was that the place smelt funny. That would have been the floor polish then.

About three hours of play was lost on the day we were at Old Trafford. It did not detract from the atmosphere though and Francis was fascinated by everything around him, even though he'd been to Trent Bridge the year before.

Surprisingly he wasn't that bothered about going home again on the Saturday morning and by the time I managed to get him in the car it was almost lunchtime.

"It's all right here, isn't it?" he said.

***

You would have thought after all those little 'Stairway to Hades' moments it would have reduced our relationship to dust. Each time it happened, a few hours, days possibly, Bella and I just carried on regardless. It sounds absurd, but it was like a ritual and we both knew the score. We both knew how to play the game.

Turning the car onto the drive on that Saturday afternoon was typical. Bella came out, smiled at both of us, hugged Francis, asked if we had had a nice time, kissed me perfunctorily on the cheek and then said. "Tea?"

We were back to normal.

Sebastian was upset that Francis had gone with me, but not him. I promised that he could come another time and to pacify him added that it wouldn't have been much fun as Francis had to do lots of fetching and carrying, moving things around, getting this and that. Francis could read between the lines too.

"If I knew Dad wanted a slave I might have thought twice," he said. Good lad.

Francis was keen to go and see grandad over at Boston again and Sebastian also wanted to come. I did ask Bella, but she declined and said that she was busy at work.

"Send him my love," as we pulled away.

It didn't take too long to get over there that morning.

"Hi Dad!" I shouted.

"Hello Grandad!" chorused the boys.

The back door was unlocked, as usual, but no sign of him. We went into the back garden and again couldn't find him. He knew we were coming. I was getting worried. We checked the shed. His car was in the driveway. There would be no point in phoning his mobile as he never took it with him, in fact it probably wasn't even charged.

"Francis, take Sebastian with you and take a walk down The Lane and see if you can see him."

The boys set off while I checked the other rooms. I'm not sure why, but I knocked on his bedroom door and then pushed it open dreading what I may discover. He was not there; I even checked the floor on the other side of the bed. I checked the bathroom and the other bedroom; nothing. As I came out of the back door again, I heard his voice in the distance.

"Hello, boys, how are you?" he called to his relieved grandsons.

He was looking over the hedge from Joe Chamberlain's place. The boys said they had come to find him. I went along The Lane to greet him too, but I gave him a hug and saying with relief, "Oh, Dad."

"I was only giving Joe some tomatoes and cucumbers, what's all the fuss about?"

I remembered that feeling from that morning as we were driving back and was troubled to think he was my only connection to my childhood, it could be gone in an instant.

***

"Poacher's?"

"Absolutely," said John. "It was hot on site today."

He'd been helping to service a pump out in the Fens for a drainage channel. It must have been hard work as they had to clear a lot of vegetation that had grown around the outlet pipe first.

The first half of the glass went quickly.

"How's Sandra?"

"More to the point, how's Bella?"

I admitted that things were no better and that we had fallen into the same old cycle of normal domestic life punctured with recriminations, blame and arguments.

Although my first response was, "She's a fucking nightmare," and then I explained the events as they unfolded.

After I got it off my chest, he confirmed that it sounded, "Like a fucking nightmare." We were in agreement then.

He and Sandra were getting on fine, and he reckoned that he might be moving in with her at Gainsborough.

"What about the house? What about Maria?"

John explained he would force the sale of the house or give Maria an ultimatum to buy out his share, after expenses of course. It was a good job they didn't have children I thought but hadn't voiced that opinion.

He went on to say, "That way, I can have some working capital while I'm in Sandra's place, see if it works out with her and then decide what's next."

"Sounds a good plan." I caught the barman's eye. "Two more 'Poacher's' please."

***

The last few months had been stressful enough without throwing a family holiday into the mix. Two and three years ago we stayed in that lovely little Norfolk cottage and last year we did lots of little excursions.

In my mind I wanted to see if we could resolve the problems in our marriage. We were not able to do it through Relate (I still smile at the incredulity of that kindly face), and we were not having much success at home. Weirdly, we would have our 'Staircase to Hades' moments and the next day she may throw back the duvet in the dark and give me a wank saying, 'I know you want it'. There's a saying isn't there, something about squaring the circle. I never really understood what that meant but presumed it was something about finding a solution to a complex problem.

I had to give it another shot with Bella, so I started the ball rolling.

"Look, there's a cottage in Marsden that is available for a few days at the end of August that sleeps four. Do you fancy getting away?"

"Is it self-catering?"

"Yes, I think so."

"So, you want a skivvy to cook, clean, wash up and do all the little jobs."

"That's not what I thought. We could go to a hotel for a few days instead then."

"What, two rooms. That will be exorbitant."

"If it is our only time away it will be worth it."

"What are we going to do in a hotel for three or four days?"

"I was thinking we could walk in the peak district, find some amusements for the boys, I don't know, there must be loads of places to visit." As I was saying this, my stomach started to knot up and I was now wondering if this was a good idea.

"I'll leave it to you then, but I don't want to end up in a cheap fleapit where the food is rubbish."

No pressure there then. I'll be honest, there was a reason for suggesting Marsden and the north peak district area, it was relatively close to Manchester. If I could get

Bella to see the flat and more of Manchester, you never know, miracles may occur.

***

Two weeks later I went back to Manchester on my own. I wanted to check on the flat and drop off a few more things, books mainly, see if the wi-fi connection had been made. I also went into the department briefly. There was no real need to do so but I liked walking the newly polished floor and taking in the smells, check my pigeonhole, look into the seminar rooms, my staff room, the lecture theatre even though they were completely deserted. It lifted my spirits.

Mid-afternoon, I picked up the phone and called Katie. "Hi"

"Hi, are you OK?"

I explained I was in Manchester and could pop over and see her and look at the loft conversion. I thought, naughtily, that I may have an opportunity to 'christen' the attic room by fucking her there. She said that it wasn't convenient today, perhaps another time. She then said that the work was all done, and she was really happy with it and thanked me.

"Have you decorated it?"

"Well, I had some help from Marcus."

Marcus? Ah, that's why it's not convenient today. She had moved on and I couldn't blame her. I still wanted to fuck her though but that was not going to happen.

***

"Welcome to The Pines," said the receptionist.

"Hello, we're Mr and Mrs Avery. We have a double and a twin room booked."

The girl was so covered in makeup I started to wonder why it didn't crack as she spoke.

"Oh yes," and then added, "Oh no. We have reserved you two twins; all our doubles have gone. I'm so sorry. We can push the twin beds together to make a double for you."

Bella said, "That was fine, we can manage as it is." There's a good start I thought.

The rooms were actually quite pleasant, and the food was what you would expect, good quality traditional food and lots of choice. We went into the restaurant and the boys were not as self-conscious as I would have been at their age.

"Chicken burger and chips," said Francis to the waitress.

"Fish fingers and chips," was Sebastian's choice.

"Dover Sole with new potatoes and seasonal vegetables," was Bella's selection.

"Lasagne, please."

***

Back in our room, Bella had to alter her usual bedtime routine as the en-suite did not provide the privacy she would have preferred. For the first time in weeks, I saw her naked form as she moved across the bedroom floor to get her nightdress. As my eyes followed her, she was aware of me looking at her.

"What?" she said.

"I was just thinking you have kept your shape really well."

"Oh, stop it."

When she climbed into her bed, I tried to slide in beside her intent on making love to her properly. You never know, a new environment, nice food, a few glasses of wine and I could be lucky. My hands went to her legs and stroked her thighs as my head dove under the duvet.

"For goodness' sake, Phil, I've a full stomach and that wine's given me a headache."

"I could try and relax you."

"I know what you want and I'm sorry it's not going to happen. I made you cum only a few days ago."

Back to reality.

***

The next day we took in the Standedge Tunnel experience and walked up to Stanza Stones Trail up by Pule Hill. The boys were not keen on walking, but the views were spectacular, and I often find myself asking why anybody would want to go abroad when all this beauty is here. Francis had the answer to that one, it's warmer in Spain.

***

The day after, I persuaded the family to come and see the flat. I actually think that Bella had done enough walking the day before. Francis was keen as he had previous knowledge and wanted to show his mum and little brother around and Sebastian was desperate to see where his dad was staying.

"If this is what Manchester is like, you can keep it," said Bella after she'd approached the flat via Princess Drive. Her attitude did not change after Francis went running around the flat announcing the rooms and what he had done when he helped me. Bella went to the window and looked out.

"Why would you want to stay here?"

"All of Manchester is not like this," I said in its defence. "I can take you to some nice areas."

"I'll make some tea," said Bella.

"Look, we can all come here for a few days and have a proper look round. I will need to sort out a put-me-up bed for Sebastian."

"Why can't I have a proper bed?" interjected my youngest.

Francis came to the rescue. "I don't mind sleeping on a camp bed."

So, three in favour, one against. But democracy doesn't work like that with Bella. I knew she wouldn't want to come back soon. Even after more than two years her reluctance was written all over her face and nothing I could say or do would break the defences down.

Well at least I have a haven here for myself.

Chapter 16

The start of term was its usual gentle introduction before the main events. My timetable was similar to last year and I was delighted with that as I could use my previous teaching material but tweak it as we go along.

During that first week we had our first meeting of the research team looking at earthquakes and how they affect building design. I was particularly keen to get involved with this as I had done no major research on any topics. Well, that's not strictly true, as Simon and I had delivered a series of lectures on structural defects, and we needed to do a lot of research for that.

The professor started the proceedings and introduced the team. Frederick Mahler was the lead as he had specialism in fluid mechanics. Frederick began by saying that during an earthquake, the soils and strata below the formation levels are so vibrated that they become fluid in nature. The fluids laboratory technicians had been conducting tests on uniform dry sand particles and pulsing longitudinal shock waves at various frequencies to observe the changes in the formation of the particles. The school of thought was that any building, low or high rise, should be considered like a boat or ship and stability was paramount.

The current thinking was that the building structure should be a rigid cage capable of resisting dynamic forces built on top of a stiff raft foundation with anti-vibration mountings. Greg was also on the team for his soil mechanics knowledge and me from our department. There would be five of us collaborating as we were to be joined by two engineering geologists from the geography department, Colin Davis and Tamsin Heel.

We were all asked to provide a summary of our qualifications, experience, relevant knowledge and levels of interests. I thought that we would have done this after the meeting on paper and submit to the lead, but no, the professor wanted us to give individual verbal presentations.

"Phil, would you like to start?" Read between the lines, 'you will start'.

Deep breath, dive in and keep going.

I outlined my career history to date and gave a synopsis of everything I thought I could offer. I did draw the group's attention to the fact that I was familiar with British Standards of design and Eurocodes, but it may be prudent to see how design criteria are employed in the various earthquake zones that we will be investigating, i.e., Turkey, Japan, Greece, San Francisco, etc.

Come up for air.

Fortunately, my resume was well appreciated and now I can sit back, relax and watch the others squirm. I was quite looking forward to hearing about Tamsin. She looked nice. She was probably mid-thirties, dark long hair tied back and bookish glasses. She had a crisp white blouse and dark blue skirt. I tried to imagine her standing up, taking off her glasses and removing her hair band and shaking her long hair wildly before walking over to me and stripping off her clothes. My fantasy could have gone further before I reminded myself that I needed to concentrate on the research team. I had clearly watched too many sex films.

***

There was one evening when I left the department, that I was in automatic mode and found myself about a quarter of a mile from David and Anna's place when I came too. Idiot. Turn right here.

I opened the door to the flat and was struck by the eerie quietness inside. There was noise of course, but from outside; the traffic, the neighbours, a few emergency vehicles rushing by, but it was quiet in here. No girls saying, 'it's Uncle Phil', no one saying, 'Only pizza tonight I'm afraid'.

Once again, I felt incredibly lonely. Can I avoid the temptation of those girls in the red-light area? Not for the first time in my life I felt sorry for myself. The logical battle was once again active in my brain. I am married to a woman who may care for me but does not love me in the way that I needed, then I have fallen in love with a married woman with two beautiful girls, I lost the love of a beautiful Jamaican girl, Katie. So, do I look for true love elsewhere? Tamsin, the earthquake specialist in our team seemed very nice, perhaps I could make the earth move for her.

**

The group of twenty-five, or so, freshers were sitting in front of me in one of the seminar rooms on their first morning in the department. Their expressions were not dissimilar to my own when I started at Bristol all those years ago and immediately, I felt an affinity to each and every one of them. There were at least five or six girls in the group and I was pleased that they were seriously interested in engineering. It was high time that any sexist barriers were broken down in a traditionally male dominated environment.

"Good morning. I'm Phil Avery and I have been asked to act as your course tutor. No, let me re-phrase that. I asked to be your course tutor as I think it is a very important role. You are new here, probably don't know many people, worried about what is expected of you, not sure how to face the challenge, am I right?"

Several heads smiled and others nodded. I went on to say they are welcome to talk to me any time when I'm free. I empathise too much sometimes but I went on to say I know exactly how they feel as I was a country boy from rural Lincolnshire thrown into University at Bristol to do a course, I was convinced I couldn't do.

"No matter how traumatised you may feel, I was worse, I promise you."

The term went on in its familiar pattern and I was able to ride along in relative comfort. I was still oscillating between Lincoln and Manchester, oscillating from my sadness at home and my self-imposed exile in the flat. There were lighter times of course. Francis did ask for help with his maths and physics, after all he was now in year eleven and the pressure was on. Even Sebastian trusted me to help him with basic algebra. John was happily shacked up with Sandra. Katie and Marcus were now a definite item, despite the fact that Katie's parents lived with her now.

I needed to do something to fill the void within the flat and decided to enrol on a calligraphy course and also to join a music society. I wanted to get back to church music but as I was in Lincoln at the weekends, I was not keen to join the church choir there. The university had a chamber choir and they practised mid-week and welcomed any members of staff as well as students.

The conductor welcomed me into the hall and introduced me to the group. There were only twenty or so singers and I felt as though I really didn't belong there. Once those initial reservations were overcome and I relaxed, I felt like I did when I was nine, that's when I first joined the church choir (again it was my father that encouraged me).

I joined the other tenors, and we sang 'Ave Maria', 'O For the wings of a dove' by Mendelsohn and finally, Parry's 'Jerusalem'.

As I drove back to the flat that night, I felt strangely comforted but something had been nagging me for several weeks and I couldn't shake off whatever the malaise was.

***

The birthday card I was writing did not say what I wanted to say. It was now late November and Imogen's birthday was on Friday of next week. I had simply written 'Happy 7th birthday Imogen'. Was it over two and a half years ago when I saw her for the first time pulling at the hem of her dress as she clutched her teddy? I needed to say more, 'My little munchkin' appeared at the bottom with three XXX's.

I put the card in the package with the coloured crayons and posted it.

***

A young girl with long dark hair knocked on our staff room door and pushed it open. "Hello, Mr Avery, can I talk to you please?"

"Sure, I am free at the moment. Well, I have a seminar in a quarter of an hour. It's Deborah, isn't it?"

"My friends call me Debbie," she said.

Both Greg and Simon were at their desks, but I sensed Debbie wanted to speak in private.

"Let's go next door," I said. "It's empty at the moment."

Once we got in, I invited her to sit at one side of a table and I sat the other.

"How can I help?"

"I want to leave the course Mr Avery and return home."

This sort of statement is not unusual and there are many reasons why students feel this way; homesickness, inability to keep up with course demands, realisation that they are on the wrong course, financial restrictions, break up of relationships, and in one case I was told about, pregnancy. I had already lost one of my students earlier in the term as he realised, he wanted to do mechanical engineering instead of civil.

"Oh, I'm sorry to hear that, Debbie. I thought you were doing really well; is there a reason you want to go?"

She explained that her father had phoned from their home in Gillingham to say that her mother had been diagnosed with breast cancer and there was a malignant tumour in her armpit. They had confirmed the type of tumour through a biopsy and the results came back yesterday. Apparently, her parents had not told her of her mother's illness before she started the course in September, they did not want to worry her unnecessarily if it was a false alarm or the tumour turned out to be benign.

Debbie went on to say that she came from a large family, there were four children, and she was the youngest. All her siblings were working but two of them were still living at home.

"What do your parents think you should do?"

"My dad says that I should stay here and see out the term. I haven't spoken to mum."

"Are you feeling as though you ought to be there, you know, to help out or something?"

"Yes, I think so. I want to be nearer my mum."

"Your dad might be right. Are they coping at home right now?"

"I think so, my big sister is there."

"It could be, Debbie, that your mum will feel very guilty that your studies have been truncated because of her. Your re-appearance now may cause her more angst. It is every parent's dream to see their child step out on their own path."

Debbie nodded along in agreement but she was clearly traumatised.

I added. "You need to be strong for your mum's sake."

Debbie agreed to stay but she would go home at the weekend as she wanted to be there. That was perfectly normal, and I told her that if she missed any lectures on Friday or Monday, I would arrange some extra sessions for her to catch up. She thanked me and got up to go.

As she was about to open the door, I said, "Debbie?"

"Mr Avery?"

"Stay strong, dear girl."

I had wanted to tell her that my own mother died ten years ago from breast cancer, but that was not appropriate nor kind. That poor girl was going to be living through her own demons in the next few months.

The next week I received a text from Anna. My heart missed a beat as it was the first time in nearly six months she had contacted me. The text said little to justify my excitement. It simply read.

Hi Phil. Thank you so much for Imogen's card and present. The girls would love to see you. Can you come here tonight on your way to the flat? A xxx

Sadly, I was going to be working until late as I had a seminar. I was surprised she suggested tonight as tomorrow was Imogen's birthday. I texted back.

Hi Anna. Great to hear from you. Been thinking a lot about the family. Am working till eight and could be there by nine, is that too late? Phil xxx

The reply was almost instant.

No, that's great. See you at nine. Thank you. A xxx

***

Walking along those familiar paving slabs brought some happy memories. The stained glass was shining brightly illuminated by the corridor lamp inside. I didn't want to ring the bell as I was sure the girls would be asleep, so I gently tapped on the door. Neither David nor Anna answered so I knocked a bit louder.

It was Anna who opened the door. She looked so pale and tired.

She just said very quietly, "Thank you so much for coming," and melted into me, her head on my chest and her hands clutching my upper arms. She added, "I'm sorry, I shouldn't have asked you."

Her smell was so familiar. I kissed the top of her head and helped her in as she seemed so frail at that moment. It reminded me of that really hot Monday back in May all those months ago when we shared cheese on toast.

I led her into the kitchen and sat her down.

"What's happened?" I asked.

She didn't answer but rested her elbows on the table and let her head fall forward into her forearms. Her long hair fell around her shoulders and masked her face.

"Where's David? Is he still at work?"

Her voice remained soft, "No."

I got her a glass of water and sat the other side of the table to wait until she was ready to talk. I wondered if she had taken something, some drugs or drunk too much perhaps, but that was not Anna. I reached over the table and took both her hands in mine. She started to cry, and it was obvious she had been crying earlier.

"Are the girls all right?" I said in a soft voice to match hers.

"Yes," she whispered. "They're asleep."

After a few minutes she looked up at me with a pained expression and sunken eyes.

Her soft voice continued. "I shouldn't be burdening you like this. I am so sorry."

"Honestly, it's OK, I'm glad you contacted me."

"Really? I thought you wanted to be away from here."

"I couldn't explain it at the time, I should be the one to apologise."

There was a brief pause. She sat back in the dining chair and looked into the middle of the tabletop between us.

"David has left us," she said softly.

"Oh my God. I am so sorry. When did this happen."

"Sometime in the summer, July, August perhaps."

"Why did you not tell me?"

"You have Bella and the boys. You don't need more stress."

If only she knew. If only she had any idea why I had to leave. At this moment in time, I could have cried too.

"Oh, Anna. If only you knew."

"Knew what?"

"How I really feel about you. You must have noticed when we sang together."

She suppressed a stifled laugh that brought even more tears to her eyes and replied. "What do we do now?"

There was no way I was leaving her that night. We talked for a while longer and I made her coffee and some toast as she hadn't eaten all day. I cleared the mess in the kitchen and did some impromptu tidying. Locking the doors, I led her upstairs and helped her into her bedroom. Oddly, I had only seen the bedroom once before when David gave Bella and I a tour around the place. She was wearing an old top and leggings so I removed her light sandals and helped her remove her top, but she kept her leggings and T-shirt on.

Covering her with the sheet and duvet, I whispered, "I will go and sleep in the attic room."

"Please stay here with me," she said.

I lay on the top of the duvet still in my suit trousers and shirt having removed my tie and jacket. I needed to be at work at nine tomorrow I told her. So I will leave early so as not to disturb the girls. I promised I will be back, and we could talk properly. She fell asleep within half an hour, so I left a note on the pillow.

I wrote simply.

You've not seen the last of me. X

I picked up my old key off the kitchen shelf and left just before midnight, returned to the flat and was euphoric for the first time in a long time.

***

It was now Friday, and after last night I could not go back to Lincoln. With Anna in such a fragile state I had to make excuses as to why I did not want to return home. I had lied before to Bella, and I wasn't proud of myself for doing so but these were extreme circumstances.

"Hi Bella. Are you OK?"

265

"Yes, are you on your way?"

"No, I've got a massive problem here."

What should I say? Two choices: One, David has left Anna and she is in a terrible state, and I need to be there for her and the girls or, two, say there's something wrong with the car?

"The fuel pump has gone and the RAC say they can't fix it, it'll need to be collected by a garage tomorrow."

"Oh, for goodness' sake. So now what?"

"Well, I'll see what I can do and phone you tomorrow."

"So, what am I supposed to tell the boys? Their dad isn't coming home. They were looking forward to seeing you."

That was unlikely as three of the last four weekends Francis was either on his iPad, playing a computer game or watching TV and Sebastian was playing at Stevie's. I just got the cursory 'Hi. Dad' and a kiss on the cheek from my wife.

I had rung Anna during the day just to check she was OK and said I'd be there this evening.

"You will need to get back to Bella," she said.

"We can talk later. Is David seeing Imogen tonight as it's her birthday?"

"No, I think he said he's in Milan at a conference or something."

***

I rang the bell and turned the key simultaneously. Stepping into the corridor, I shouted, "Happy Birthday, Munchkin!"

"Uncle Phil." Imogen ran and put her arms around me. Jasmine came into the corridor but was a little reticent as I had been away so long.

"Hi sweetie, how are you?"

"Good, thank you, Uncle Phil."

Stepping through the door to the kitchen I was surprised to see Katie, and presumably, Marcus, having tea with Anna. Anna explained that Katie and Marcus had popped in to see the birthday girl. Anna introduced me to Marcus and I wondered how much he knew about me and Katie, or then again, how much Anna knew about me and Katie. Everybody seemed convivial so I presumed Katie had not said anything. Marcus was tall with curly blond hair and was more Katie's age, I wondered how fit he was because he would certainly need to be!

We talked for a quarter of an hour or so and the two of them left. I'm sure Katie winked at me in the corridor, I did kiss her on the cheek. She was, after all, a great girl.

As Anna shut the door, she leaned back against it. We said nothing for a moment as the girls were still marauding around but the eye contact was constant, and the smiles were unmistakeable. She looked so much better than yesterday evening.

"Thank you so much for coming to see me last night. I feel much better now. Also, thank you for coming to see Imogen today. It will mean a lot to her that you've come."

"I had no choice."

She stopped talking for a moment, looked at the floor and sighed heavily then said, "Now you need to leave."

What did she say? Why did she say that?

"Anna?"

"You need to get back to Bella, she and the boys need you and I would never forgive myself."

"Anna, please. Can we talk about…" she interrupted me.

"Come and see the girls next week, please."

She opened the door to let me out, but I wanted to say goodbye to the girls properly and tell them I will see them next week. I called back to the main part of the house.

"Girls, I'm in a bit of a rush tonight but will it be OK if I come and see you next week?"

"Oh, do you have to go Uncle Phil?" said Imogen.

"Apparently, I do."

Take that deep breath and keep on going.

Chapter 17

"We weren't expecting you until tomorrow," Bella said.

"Managed to get it fixed in the end. Apparently, it was some dirt that was caught in the carburettor and not the fuel pump." The lie was complete. Bella knew nothing about cars, I could have said anything.

That weekend was the worst I had felt for a very long time. My chest was tight, my stomach was knotted (there were no butterflies this time), my mouth kept going dry and I had this desperate feeling of wanting to flee but was tied down, chained down, trapped. I found myself pacing up and down the garden for no reason, looking at my phone for messages constantly, unable to concentrate. I now felt like a timber wolf pacing up and down in its cage, a canary in an aviary, a dog chained to its kennel. Helpless. Vulnerable.

At one point, I picked up the vinyl album I had had since my university days 'The lamb lies down on Broadway' by Genesis. I wasn't intending to play it but looked at the sleeve cover as it depicted my situation right now. It is the story of a poor Puerto Rican boy, Rael, from the Bronx. There are three photos of him on the cover, in the first he is imprisoned and in the third he is free next to a mountain stream. The middle photo shows him agonising how to free himself of the shackles as his conscience wages a battle in his mind. At that particular moment it perfectly captured how I felt.

As you can imagine sleep became difficult to achieve but welcome when it did. Sometime during Saturday, I had to plan an escape.

Over lunch I said to Bella. "I will need to go back to Manchester tomorrow evening. I have to be in early on Monday morning," was my first move.

"Why can't you just get up earlier?"

"I need to give a presentation for the research." Next move.

"You can do that tomorrow."

"All my paperwork is in the flat." Check.

"Why didn't you bring it back, you normally do."

"With all the trouble with the car, I left it behind." Checkmate.

I was not happy telling a double lie but pleased with myself for combining the two so seamlessly. Fundamentally, I am not a devious person and it chewed me up inside to recognise that this situation is driving me into a place I am not at all comfortable.

***

By the time I got to Anna's on Sunday evening it was later than I had planned. I just hoped she hadn't gone to bed early.

I tapped on the door. No answer.

Tapped louder. No answer.

I had my key still; do I use it? I don't want to startle her by just entering unexpectedly. I phoned her instead.

"Phil?"

"Hi, Anna, do you mind me phoning? I'm sorry to ring late."

"Well, it's only half eight. It's good to hear you. Are you OK?"

"Yes, but I wanted to hear your voice." At that moment I leaned forward and rang the doorbell.

"Hang on Phil, there's someone at the front door."

"Oh, really?"

"Can I ring you back?"

"Sure," and hung up and waited.

After a few seconds I heard the door being unlocked and she stood there framed by the light coming from the corridor.

"Oh Phil. I don't believe it. What are you doing here?" It wasn't said in any way accusatory but with genuine relief. "Come in."

"I need to tell you something and it's important, to me."

"What is it?"

I didn't need to take a deep breath this time and it didn't matter what happened next because now I can be my true self. I stepped inside, closed the door and took her in my arms.

"I am really deeply, deeply in love with you."

"Oh Phil, I love you too. I think I always have ever since we first met."

"Surely, that was back in Lincoln when we first sang together?"

"I know," she said "What are we going to do now? We have to be careful there are too many people who are going to get hurt."

"Why do you think I left at the end of last year? I thought you and David were happy. I love the girls and I could not be the reason their parents split up."

"I feel the same about Francis and Sebastian. And Bella of course." She added after a pause.

Clearly, we had so much to discuss and think about. We would try and find the right path. We will make this work, somehow. Right now, I wanted her to know that I was genuine. I kissed her so gently, stroked her face with my fingertips, kissed her eyelids, her nose and that delicate chin before discovering the nape of her neck.

The sexual tension was so powerful for both although we both knew that we couldn't take that next step, not yet. We were as strongly pragmatic as we were desperate for each other. My trembling hands had continued to caress her and had moved over her breasts, her waist and her buttocks.

"Oh, my God," she said in a mock rebuke. "You are terrible. Come on, sit down let's talk this through."

We agreed that I will stay in the flat this week, but I will pop in for a couple of evenings to see the girls and have dinner together, then we will be able to talk some more. Anna needed to know more about what was happening between Bella and me. She really wanted to know if there was a chance that Bella and I could be reconciled. She thought that if there was a chance, I should investigate every avenue. In my mind, I thought I had done so, although I didn't voice that.

"Come tomorrow for dinner," Anna said.

By eleven a.m. the next morning, I was showered, dressed and standing in front of the second-year students for Structural Design 1 and it was the first lecture on reinforced concrete beams. It was the material for which I had the most design experience. I took the students through the process of finding the bending moment, breadth of beams and effective depth that would lead them to the percentage of the tension steel area required. Then I showed them how to design shear reinforcement using links or bent up bars and finally, deflection check. I was able to wrap up the lecture with seconds to spare of the hour and a half. I was walking on air this morning and I'm sure the students noticed.

As I followed behind three or four of them in the corridor I heard one saying, "Mr Avery was on fire today."

He certainly was.

***

Ringing the bell and turning the key was now something of a well-rehearsed ritual.

"Any munchkins in residence?"

Two of them were and they ran to greet me. Anna had tipped them off.

"Pizza?" Anna said.

"Couldn't be better."

That night after we had put the girls to bed gave us time to talk. I heard from Anna about what had happened in the summer when David decided to leave. Apparently, he had been unhappy in the marriage for some considerable time, years probably, he was expecting Anna not to move with him when they relocated from Aberdeen and then again when he took up the post in Manchester from Lincoln.

"But that was before Imogen was born, surely?" I said.

"Yes, he said it was a mistake and didn't want more after Jasmine. I am not sure he wanted children in the first place."

"Well, Imogen was a beautiful mistake," I murmured.

During the last few years, David had been having an affair and it was why he was often late home or didn't come back at all. I thought my life was complicated but I kept that thought to myself. Anna went on to say that these so-called conferences didn't exist, or if they did, he used it as an opportunity to go away with his mistress. I thought that was an old fashioned term 'mistress' but Anna used it without malice or jealousy. Everything came to a head when his mistress needed more commitment from David. He wanted to finally break away from Anna and live with his new woman back in Oxford. Anna was unable to tell me much because she only heard some of this through the grapevine.

I asked, "So who is she?" I felt stupid at my insensitivity. "Sorry, Anna that was tactless."

"It's all right, I have accepted it now, but it still hurts."

I waited for her to lead the conversation as my thoughtlessness could only cause more upset.

"Her name is Felicity, and she was David's first love back in Oxford. They have been in close contact ever since Felicity left her partner a few years ago."

I gave out a sigh which was a mix of irony and disbelief. "Can you believe it?"

"Believe what?" she said.

"All this time I have been in love with you and David has been planning to escape."

She gave out a small hollow laugh. "It does explain his reluctance to commit fully to our marriage. It's been going on for years and I kept excusing it."

"Why did you put up with it?"

"I am his wife, and I made my vows, I guess. Sorry, does that sound old fashioned and pathetic?"

"No, quite honourable, actually."

We sat quietly for a while as we both considered the words, we had used to each other. Anna made a cup of coffee for the two of us and she composed herself again. We were both fundamentally serious people, and our wedding vows would be significant for us. I did not believe that I could ever contemplate separation and divorce from Bella, and I am sure Anna was the same about David. After a while she sat down at the dining table and stared into the middle distance and started talking again.

"The worst was when he left."

Anna described that fateful day when he told her he was leaving, and it sounded horrific. David came back in the middle of the day during the summer and announced he was leaving, collected his essential belongings and said he would come back for the rest when it was convenient. All the time this happened the girls were traumatised and kept screaming, 'don't go daddy'.

"That's horrendous," was my pathetic response. It did explain Jasmine's reluctance to greet me last week in her normal way. Perhaps she thought that the men in her life could not be trusted. What the hell am I going to say to Sebastian and Francis when the time comes?

Anna must have picked up on my train of thought.

"What are you thinking? Is it about Bella?" she asked.

"Actually, I was thinking of the boys."

"It is why I said to you last night that so many people are going to get hurt."

"Anna, whatever happens, however difficult, however rough the road becomes, I want to be with you."

She smiled and got up from the dining table and hugged me while I sat there taking in her smell and nuzzled between her breasts. I stayed there for as long as possible until she broke the silence.

"Phil," she said. "I can't sleep with you. Not yet anyway. I am worried about Bella, and I will be thinking of her."

I understood what she said and I respected her for putting others first. We agreed, for the girl's sake if nothing else, that I would sleep in the flat and make our plans gently.

"You will have to go back on Friday to see Bella and the boys," Anna said.

"Not necessarily, I could stay here and say I'm busy."

The coward in me was never far away as I hated confrontations. Perhaps, if I had confronted Bella's unreasonable behaviour years ago I could have sailed a different path. I knew I loved Bella, quite deeply as it happens, but that love had been eroded away over years with the 'Stairway to Hades' moments, the constant criticism, the rejections and the lack of interest in anything I did at work. The only thing that kept us together was the boys and the singing, but I had lost interest in the latter in recent years. Whatever traumas she experienced as a child were so securely locked away and would never see the light of day, even if it meant the end of her marriage.

There was one episode that stuck in my mind which typified Bella's attitude to me. It came one winter morning after a large fall of snow. We didn't have Sebastian then and Francis was only a toddler. I had gone out to clear the driveway of snow, slipped, fell in stages trying to keep some balance but fell heavily on my left hip directly onto an exposed kerb stone. It hurt like hell, but Bella stood in the doorway laughing uproariously. To her, it was the funniest thing she had seen. Even after the extent of my injury was known, she couldn't stop giggling. A few days later she regaled the choral group by recollecting the images of me falling like a drunken octopus.

"Each journey starts with a single step." Anna was citing Confucius now.

"You're right, but it's not easy."

"I know," she said reassuringly.

Everything was all right with the flat when I popped in on Friday afternoon. I hadn't been back this week as I had spent each night in the attic. Anna and I were very disciplined with each other, and I did not want to compromise her by having intercourse (that's interesting, I may have used the word 'fuck' or 'screw' before) but it was different with her somehow. We did cuddle each and every night though. There was one night, Anna fell asleep and woke at five a.m. and beetled downstairs before the girls were awake. I was unaware of this as I was in a deep sleep.

***

If I was putting off the arrival in Lincoln, it wasn't really a conscious decision or action, but I had dithered in the flat for longer than needed and drove my way back along the M62 and M180. This is not a route I used often, but I presumed I did so for two reasons, firstly, it was longer and would delay me further and secondly, I could rehearse what I was going to say to Bella.

No rehearsal of this nature ever comes to fruition.

"You're late today," were Bella's first words "Can you go and pick up Sebastian, he's at Stevie's."

I reversed the car back off the drive and headed towards Stevie's house. It was less than a mile.

After knocking on the door, Stevie's dad appeared and said that the boys were playing upstairs.

"Come on, Sebastian!" I shouted.

Stevie's dad asked how things were going in Manchester. I didn't have any desire to tell him about my work and all the complications that had accrued so I simply said, "Fine, thanks."

In the car with Sebastian, I reflected on my ambivalence towards Stevie's dad and thought I had been a bit standoffish or rude even. Was I getting stronger?

How can it be that you can never find the right time to have conversations like this? Friday evening was filled with bits of trivia, half-finished chats about mundane matters, helping the boys with schoolwork, loading and unloading the dishwasher, doing my laundry from the previous week and so on.

In bed after the usual ritual, in the dull glow of the street lights I lay behind Bella with her back covered by her cotton nightdress and thought of her body. She still had a good figure, a little more wholesome but nevertheless, good. Should I try and fuck her, just one last time? I could then store the memory of the last fuck in the knowledge that she would be unaware that this will be the last time my cock enters her and fills her with my sperm. I gave myself a good talking to then, telling myself it was just spite and not love. What would Anna think if she knew I had pushed deep into Bella's vagina and humped her like a sex starved dog?

I went into the bathroom and had a wank.

Saturday was filled with the usual things; shopping, visiting her mum and dad, collecting stuff for my in-laws (soon to be my out-laws), lunch, playing footie, dinner, watching TV.

Back in bed again and I was relieved that I wasn't sexually frustrated.

Then Sunday. It has to happen today, but how? I did actually think about writing her a letter and leaving it for her to find on Monday morning. Is that not cruel? Does she not deserve better? We had been together twenty years and the ending should be more dignified, shouldn't it?

I wrote her a letter and left it on the kitchen table as I made my way westwards early on Monday morning.

Bella.

It seems strange to be writing this, but I am finding it difficult to find the words to say how I am feeling right now.

I am so depressed with how our relationship has deteriorated to the point where we barely tolerate each other. I was hoping that we may have grown old and grey together in love, but it feels as though we have gone even further apart.

I have taken a few of my things with me and I will be staying in Manchester for the foreseeable future until we can find a resolution to this mess. If you want me to remove

*the rest of my things, then I will arrange to collect them
when it is convenient to you.*

    Phil X

I felt obliged to put a token X, but declined to say, 'Dear
Bella' and 'love' at the bottom. It was short and I hadn't
mentioned the boys so that will have to be a discussion for
the future.

Am I a rat? I had gone around the house secretly
stashing the things I would need, more clothes, toiletries,
shoes, ties, suits, memory sticks with data from my PC. I
did this at various times over the weekend when they had
gone shopping or when Bella was in the kitchen and then
putting them in the boot of the car.

Paul Simon sang '50 ways to leave your lover'. I
couldn't find one.

***

It was on the A57 beyond Sheffield when the inevitable
occurred. The phone rang from home. Do I answer it now
or talk to her later? If I leave it until later, I could be with
Anna.

"Hi."

"That was cruel and despicable of you. How dare you
just leave that letter like that. We had the weekend together
and you've said nothing. Everything has been normal and
then you do that. How could you? HOW COULD YOU?"

"Look, I've been unhappy for…"

"So why didn't you tell me? We could discuss it like normal human beings."

"But when we do start talking…"

"When did you talk? You say nothing and then walk away. I know what this is about. It's why you got the flat. You've been planning this all along. Silly cow at home waiting patiently won't know what's going on. I will tell you what you are. You are a bastard."

Then she hung up. I knew what was going to happen next and starting counting, by the time I got to eight the phone rang again.

"Hi."

"Come back now. The boys will be at school in an hour, and we can talk."

"I am delivering a lecture this morning."

"Ring them and tell that you're ill. I will ring them for you," she said.

"No. I am not going to let a hundred and twenty students down."

"But you're going to let me down?"

"I would be happy to talk but when we are both in a calm state and not so hysterical."

That was the wrong thing to say.

"HYSTERICAL? My husband of twenty years gets up calmly and fucks off without saying anything. You really are a bastard." She hung up again. I counted but she didn't ring back this time.

In the car park I texted her.

Sorry. I will ring this evening when I am in the flat. x

She didn't reply.

My lecture on concrete columns didn't go as well as last week as I had that tight chest and knotted stomach again but for different reasons to last weekend. Fortunately, the students were not aware of my below par performance, but Simon did notice later as I had gone a bit quiet in our staff room.

"Are you OK, Phil?"

"Er, yes, sorry."

"You're not your usual self," he continued.

"Fancy a coffee?"

Over coffee in the staff rest area, I told Simon about my separation from Bella but left out the words 'cruel', 'despicable' and 'bastard' in the conversation I'd had with Bella. He was a good listener but that's all he could do. I wasn't expecting any pearls of wisdom, but it was good to get it off my chest. Well, partially off my chest because the sodding pain was still there.

***

I swear these paving slabs are more uneven. I rang the bell and turned the key in the lock and was back in the familiar surroundings of Anna's corridor.

"Hello!" I called.

It was David who replied. "Hello, Phil."

"David, how the devil are you?" I said this with more genuine concern than I had intended.

"Fine, thanks, busy as usual."

My mind was spinning now and going into overdrive. Where was Anna? The girls? Are they all right? Why was David here? Have they made up? Shit.

"Yes, I've had a busy time too. I gather you were at a conference in Milan. Were you a guest contributor?"

"No, not on this occasion."

Anna appeared at the kitchen door and said fairly flatly. "Hi Phil. How are you?"

I could see she was stressed but I couldn't see how to get this situation resolved. If he's back, then I should go. If he's not, then I should go and wait for Anna to phone when he's left.

"I'm OK, how are the girls?"

"They're upstairs reading or doing homework. David and I were discussing a few things."

I simply said, "Sorry to disturb. I was on my way back to the flat and thought I'd pop in to say hello. Just give me a ring whenever."

I turned and went back to the door and opened it. As I stepped out, Anna called.

"Sorry, Phil."

As I got back into the car, I felt quite weak and shaky. What the hell do I do now? If they have been reconciled and she has taken him back where does that leave me?

Chapter 18

Opening the flat door after driving from Anna's, I was aware of that stale smell that greeted me when I first got the keys. I flung open a few windows and thought about something to eat but there was nothing fresh in the place other than cans of baked beans and some cream crackers. They'll have to do.

I phoned Bella.

"Are you all right, Bella?" That was a particularly weak opening.

"What do you think?"

"Sorry, that was lame. Look, if you feel calm enough to talk now, we can. I wasn't suggesting it was all over in my letter. It was a statement of fact."

"That's not how I read it," she said. "You are 'staying in Manchester for the foreseeable future' sounds pretty much over."

"How are the boys?"

"Don't change the subject. They are all right, I haven't said anything to them, they think it's an ordinary Monday."

"Bella, you must accept things are not great. It was only a few weeks ago you said, 'you hated me and to go back to Manchester' and you pushed me away."

"I was upset, couldn't you see that?"

"I don't know why you are upset; you never tell me anything. You accuse me of not saying how I feel, but you do exactly the same thing."

There was a brief pause and then she said, "We're not going to sort this out on the phone. Come back and we can talk properly."

I said I would but not until the end of the week. My heart sank. Where is this all going?

The evening wore on and I was hoping that Anna might have phoned to tell me what was happening between her and David. My imagination was going wild, and I thought of him laying on top of her, fucking her and the sounds of his grunts were being replayed in my mind like water torture. Shall I take a drive to the red-light area? Find a girl who will help me blank this out?

I was hungry so I felt justified going to get a kebab. I remembered that shop on the corner of the main road where I stopped two years ago. As I parked the car, I looked up and down the street to see if any of those girls were working tonight. Nothing. Then a black face appeared at my window, and it was a young man in a hoody. He had it pulled up over his head and knocked rapidly on the window. Stupidly, I wound the window down, cursing my own natural trust in anybody I meet in any environment. These are, potentially, rough areas and I'd been told to avoid them, but I wasn't sure if this was such an area.

"What do you want?" he said quickly and almost menacingly.

"Sorry?"

"Crack, skunk, weed, puff?" His shopping list seemed extensive.

"No, mate, sorry, I don't need anything. I've come to get a kebab."

"Fucking prick." Was his parting shot as he moved down the shady street to look for other customers.

For a moment, it felt like a bucket of cold water had been thrown over me. I started the car and went to an area which I knew was safer territory. I had never tried drugs before, not even in Bristol, in that moment, the temptation to escape the horror I was experiencing beckoned. Escape into an intoxication of cannabis that would engulf me, take the sodding pain away, let me float into some transcendental plain above the cruel terrain and become free of everything that tormented me and take me to a safe haven.

If only. It wasn't long before the boring, middle aged, middle class country boy within me got a grip. Parking outside the Indian Ocean Takeaway just down the road from Princess Drive, I felt safe again as I entered the lurid blue, fluorescent portal to be greeted by a familiar face.

"Hello again, sir. What can I get you?" I always thought that Indian people are so courteous.

"Chicken Biryani and a plain Naan, please."

Once back in the flat, I only managed a few forkfuls of the Biryani. It was really tasty, and I normally love

Indian food, but my appetite had gone, and an empty stomach was actually filled with butterflies.

It was late, but eventually Anna texted.

Hi Phil, sorry, will ring you sometime soon. Hope you are OK. A xxx

So, they've made up then. Why would she not have said more? Fuck, fuck, fuck and other swear words at very close centres.

***

Being back in work was a great distraction, even though I felt chewed up and spat out, I was functioning well in front of my students.

"Good afternoon, everyone. How are you all doing?"

Some of the students nodded, others muttered 'fine' or 'OK'. That was a good enough rapport to get going.

"Today in surveying, I want to show how to design transition curves."

I loved teaching surveying techniques and bringing in the applied mathematics needed to demonstrate how the theory can be brought into practice. I started by asking them if they had noticed that slip roads off motorways start fairly straight and as they approach a roundabout at the end, the radius of the curve becomes smaller. It is to do with the relative velocity of vehicles travelling from high speed to slow speed approaches to enter a roundabout or a junction.

Hence the radius of the curve gradually changes from infinity to a shorter distance, hence a transitional curve. I also showed them how the curves incorporate a gradual application of super-elevation to counteract centrifugal force.

I continued. "Sometimes these transitional curves are also referred to as Euler spirals." I couldn't resist adding, "Some people believe that Euler was German, but in fact he was Swiss."

***

I rang my dad that evening.

"Hello, Dad"

"Who's that?"

"You only have one child!" I remonstrated.

"Phil? Sorry, I didn't hear what you said at the beginning."

Don't tell me he's going deaf as well as batty.

"Dad, this is going to sound weird. But can I come and stay with you at the bungalow over the weekend?"

"What, the whole family?"

"No, Dad, just me. It's complicated."

"Whatever is going on, son?"

I did not want to give dad the whole story, how could I? I didn't know myself what the hell I was going to be doing. I did tell him that Bella and I were going through a rough patch, and we needed time to sort ourselves out. He agreed, very reluctantly, but was not pleased at this intrusion and less pleased that I was suggesting that Bella and I were separating. He and mum were together for nearly forty years before she passed away. He was quite old fashioned about couples splitting up, saying that people should work harder at their marriages. I did say if he was uncomfortable about it all, I would make alternative arrangements.

"You should talk to Bella properly," he said firmly. "Go back there and talk."

"All right, Dad."

We talked about work for a while and then hung up. So, dad thinks I should go back home and talk to Bella. Perhaps he's right.

***

The phone rang just a few times.

"Hello, John."

"Hello, Phil, nice surprise."

"John, this is going to sound weird. But can I come and stay with you at Gainsborough over the weekend?"

"Er, yes, I don't think Sandra will mind. Actually, she was looking forward to meeting you sometime and she's off this weekend."

So that's settled. I arranged to get over on Saturday morning after spending Friday night in the flat. I can then meet Bella at some neutral location between Gainsborough and Lincoln, Saxilby perhaps.

The next phone call was to the 'King William' just outside Saxilby.

"Good evening, King William, can I help you?" she said sweetly.

"Hi, my name is Phil Avery, is it possible to book a table for two at six p.m. this coming Saturday?"

"Er, yes, we can do that. Can I have a phone contact?"

I gave her my telephone number and hung up.

So that bit's settled.

The next phone call was to Bella. Stand up for this call. Take a deep breath, dive in and keep going. She answered the phone.

"Hi." Her greeting was very flat.

"Do you still want to talk at the weekend?"

"Well, that's what we agreed. Are you about to tell me you are staying there and we're going to talk on the phone again?"

"No, I've booked a table on Saturday at Saxilby for 6 p.m. for the two of us. Do you think mum and dad will look after the boys for a while?"

"Saxilby? Why can't we talk when you get back here?"

Take another big breath.

"I am not coming back this weekend, but I am prepared to meet you face-to-face. We need to be away from the house to talk properly."

"Oh, for God's sake, this is getting ridiculous."

"I'm sorry, but at the moment that's all I am prepared to do."

"What am I to say to the boys? Dad's left us and he won't be seeing them again?"

"Let me talk to Francis," I said.

"No, he's in bed. I will tell them something."

It was only nine p.m. and I knew full well Francis would be procrastinating about going to bed at this time, but I let it go. We talked for a bit longer, but it was very strained and both of us were stressed. I wondered if we could combine the stress and strain to see if we could establish a value for the Modulus of Elasticity of Modern Marriages. Even I thought that was ridiculous and so I let it go.

It was all set for Saturday, even though I had manoeuvred all of this, I was very reluctant to go through with it all. I dreaded the thought that her tactical legal mind will have me wrapped up in a spider's web completely bound, unable to move and surrendering to her will and demands. The male spider is finally going to be eaten alive.

***

It wasn't until Friday morning that I got a text message from Anna. Again, my heart skipped a beat or two and my excitement soon turned to despair when I recalled that they had reconciled.

Hi Phil. So sorry for not being able to talk. Are you free? A xxx

I had two seminars on Friday morning, but I should be free after one p.m. I texted back in a very non-committal way.

Hi Anna. Busy until one, then free. Phil x

Almost immediately the phone pinged again.

Hi. Are you heading to Lincoln straight away? Can you pop in? A xxx

I had decided that I would probably not go there while David was around. I am not sure I am strong enough for that.

Of course, I went. I still wanted to see Anna and the girls even if David was there. I'll just have to be grown up and mature about it.

***

I walked up the paving slabs to that familiar door and this time I just rang the bell. Anna opened it and smiled warmly and said, "I am so, so sorry."

"Is David here?" I said in a hushed voice as I didn't want to be placed in yet another embarrassing situation.

"No."

"I realised that you must have got back together again."

"No, no, nothing like that." She seemed horrified at the thought.

"Well, what then?"

"Come in."

Once in, she reached up on tip toes and went to kiss me. I turned away.

"What's going on?" I asked.

"Oh, Phil, I'm sorry. I had no way of saying."

It turned out that David turned up on Monday, virtually unannounced, as he had taken five days holiday to sort out his personal effects and affairs: legal documents, alimony payments, child support arrangements, mortgage details, documents and emails from both his PC and co-ordinated everything onto his new laptop. He had been around the house to collect and pack all his other belongings and had them collected by a courier. He also took the girls out on a couple of occasions. Over the past week, he insisted on staying in the house, as he co-owned it and had slept in the other spare bedroom. I must admit, I was relieved he hadn't slept in the attic.

"Why did you not text or tell me? I've been going through hell these last few days."

"I'm sorry. David can be very controlling. He would look at my phone when he got an opportunity, go through my texts, emails and any correspondence. I wasn't sure what to say to you which could not have been misconstrued."

"Where is he now?"

"He's gone back to Oxford to be with that woman."

"Felicity? Is that where is living?"

"He'd secretly arranged to get a post at the John Radcliffe Hospital back in June."

"You didn't know?"

"No."

"Oh, Anna, if only you knew what I've been going through. I nearly became a drug addict because of you."

"What?"

Now I could laugh. She pretended to beat her fists on my chest and laughed too. I told her about the letter I left Bella and what my plan is for the weekend. She felt it was a bit unfair to leave a letter but clearly understood why I had done it. I will stay with John tomorrow, see Bella at a neutral location and come back on Sunday.

"Are you not going back to Lincoln now?" she asked.

"No, I am staying in the flat. I've got some Biryani to finish."

"I wasn't sure when David was leaving until this morning, so I have arranged for a childminder to look after the girls until six."

"Do you mean that you are on your own now until six?"

It was that look she gave me when we had that hug after singing the duet. Her eyes were wide, and she was biting her lower lip. All I know is that I wanted her more than ever. I could see from her eyes that she wanted me too.

Without saying another word, I led her upstairs by the hand. She then took my hand and moved towards her bedroom door pushing it open. I stopped her. She looked puzzled for a moment. I then pulled her upward to my staircase to the attic. She said nothing, nor I. Making her stand still in the middle of the room, I undressed her and prevented her from removing anything herself. All the time I tried to maintain eye contact. I was still fully dressed in my suit and tie; she was completely naked in front of me. She was so beautiful.

Lowering her on to the bedspread, I sensed she would give herself completely to me. Her eyes were wide, and she trembled, not from cold but from anticipation. That afternoon we would make love for the first time, I mean love as it transcended sex. I kissed her all over, stroked her gently, ran my fingers around her delicate features, her nose, her forehead, her chin. My kisses followed the same paths. I kissed her nape, her breasts, her toes, feet, legs and eventually parted her knees and allowed my tongue to taste her amongst her fair hair. As gently as possible I parted her lips and my tongue danced delicately over her clitoris hood. Looking up along her body she was biting the inside of her arm with eyes closed and breathing deeply. I was determined to show her she was special and continued until she shook uncontrollably and was pulling away in ecstasy and panting with little moans of pleasure. I took her ankles and pulled her across to the side of the bed, spread her legs and knelt on the floor between them. Undoing my belt and fly, I took out my rampant self and pushed into her for the first time. She lay panting with her eyes closed. I wanted to move slowly back and forth but the excitement was too much, and I pushed fast and deep into her. Her head was to one side and her eyes closed.

I said, "Have the decency to look at me while I am fucking you."

The animal instinct hadn't left me altogether then. Her eyes seemed even wider as she fixed me with her gaze, her facial expression serious and her mouth slightly open as she panted at each thrust.

After the inevitable roar of the wild animal from within, I stayed in her to allow my cream to seep deep into her. It was only then that I removed my tie and jacket.

Breathing heavily, she asked, "What was that?"

"I wanted to show you how much I love you."

"That was amazing, I've never felt like that before. What did you do to me?"

"Are you still feeling tingly?"

"Yes. That can't have been legal."

"I think you came."

"I've never come anything like that before."

I bent forward to kiss her gently on her lips and face while cradling her head in my hands.

For the next three hours we stayed in my bed amongst the crumpled sheets and duvet. The bedspread lay discarded on the floor, and we alternated between caressing each other and dozing off in a satisfied and euphoric state.

Later, I wanted to make her come again and nuzzled my head between her legs, but she stopped me saying, "Oh, no, I'm still sensitive there."

I just smiled happily at my achievement.

I can take on the world with my bare hands now. If I was losing resolve about this coming weekend I was now fully energised.

Chapter 19

The rest of the Biryani tasted all the better this evening. Anna and I agreed that we would not complicate matters or confuse the girls by me staying there. I left before the childminder delivered Jasmine and Imogen back and went to the flat.

I would leave in the morning at about ten a.m. and it will only take a couple of hours to get to John and Sandra's. There will be time to have a pint and a heart to heart with John before I set off to meet Bella. Despite my newfound strength and determination, I sensed it was going to be a difficult evening tomorrow. There is no manual or instruction leaflet for this eventuality. John and Maria's separation was quite torrid despite their prior and well-rehearsed agreement. Maria's insensitivity by bringing men back to her bedroom to satisfy her sex drive caused John no end of angst and distress. David and Anna's separation was a complete shock as he just announced it as a 'fait accompli' and caused no end of damage to Anna and the girls. I wonder how that trauma may affect the girl's mental health in the future.

Oh well, Phil and Bella's separation will take whatever course it needs to go.

**

I had a massive realisation that Friday evening that I was concentrating solely on Bella and had forgotten the impact it may have on Francis and Sebastian. I phoned Anna.

"Hello," she said.

"What colour knickers are you wearing?" I enquired, then quickly saying, "Shit, are you on speaker phone?"

She laughed. "No, I'm not. Anyway, you'll have to guess."

Well, I remembered they were pink this afternoon when I removed them.

"Pink," I said triumphantly.

"No."

"No?"

"White. The pink ones got very damp.."

We both felt warm about the memory of that afternoon. Now I needed to be serious for a while.

"Anna. I have forgotten about the boys."

"What do you mean?"

"What is going to happen to the boys after Bella and I separate?"

It started a very long conversation, and we thought it may work if I arranged to have the boys come and stay with Anna and I in her house. A week or two during holidays, perhaps a weekend once a month. She was convinced the girls would accept me living with them without any difficulty. In fact, she knew they would love

299

that. I could let the flat go and move in with her. We could buy out David's share of the house eventually. All things were possible, and Anna could help me steer a course which made sense.

"I love you, Anna."

"I love you too."

"No, what I mean is, I really love you."

"Oh, I hope it all works as well as possible tomorrow," she said.

"Anna? Are you still tingly?"

"You are terrible!"

***

Sandra's little house was much smaller than I had anticipated as it was a Victorian mid-terrace, two up, two down with a 1960's extension housing the kitchen and bathroom tacked onto the back.

"Hello, you must be Sandra," I said as she opened the door.

First impressions often count, and my initial thoughts were that she was nothing like Maria. Whereas Maria would not be seen dead without her makeup, not a hair out of place and dressed to the nines, the woman in front of me wore a loose-fitting top and slacks and as if she had just checked the tyre pressures on their Vauxhall.

"And you must be Phil. I've heard a lot about you. Come on in, John won't be long."

Sandra made some coffee, showed me around the house and garden, which didn't take long, and we filled the time talking about her job as an assistant manager for a local convenience store. She went on to say she works every other weekend, but this was her weekend off. She wanted to know more about what I did.

"John says you teach building."

It was a bit more complicated than that, so I just said, "Yes, that's right. Actually, it was John who alerted me to the vacancy. If it hadn't been for him, I wouldn't be in this God-awful mess."

The irony and sarcasm were lost on her and I thought it was rather unfair of me to play silly games. I backtracked.

"No, I didn't mean it like that. I mean that John has been an absolute star and helped me tremendously. He's one of life's good guys."

She smiled at the warmth of my testimony.

"Hi, Phil!" shouted John from the front door. "Sorry, I wasn't here when you arrived. I've been to a site at Sleaford, getting ready for some de-watering starting on Monday."

He turned to Sandra and gave her a quick hug with his left arm while extending his right hand to shake my hand and kissed Sandra on the forehead. I am glad he didn't get that the wrong way round.

"Coffee?" Sandra said to John.

John looked at me. "Or would you like something stronger?"

I replied. "No coffee is great. I probably need to keep a clear head for this evening."

"Good idea, there aren't many great pubs round here anyway," said John.

Sandra cut up a pork pie, some cheese, tomatoes, pickles, bread and olives. She laid them on the dining table for a communal help yourself as we sat around talking. We spent the early afternoon chatting about so many things; John's work, Sandra's work, Sandra's three grown up children, Maria, Sandra's ex, John's house, John's plans for the future, Anna and the girls, David, my flat in Manchester, Francis and Sebastian, and of course, Bella. It was nice to get Sandra's female perspective, even though she had never met Bella. She thought Bella had not been fair in digging her heels in against the move to Manchester, especially as she had, albeit reluctantly, agreed to the re-location. I left out all the problems in our sex life. Eventually, Sandra, who looked at John at the time, held his hand and said something like, "If you truly love your man, then you'd do anything for him," then she added, "and if a man truly loves his woman, he will do the same."

What a great girl, I thought. She should be elected to parliament and sit in the cabinet as minister for marriage and relationships.

**

That feeling of butterflies in the stomach, the tightness of the chest and slight palpitations accompanied me along the

A156 to Saxilby. I was, perhaps cowardly, hoping she wouldn't show. She had made excuses for things she didn't want to do in the past. 'I couldn't find a babysitter at this late stage', 'you hadn't confirmed it was definitely happening', 'Sebastian's running a temperature', 'my dad's taken a turn for the worse'. No such luck, as I turned into the King William car park, her car was there already. She waited until I got out of my car before she opened her door.

"Hi," I said, trying to find a middle ground between warmth and neutrality.

"I still don't understand why you've dragged me all this way. Why are we doing this?" she said, kissing me on the cheek less perfunctory than normal.

She had made an effort tonight as she looked great. Not too much makeup, knee length skirt with a blue wrap around style blouse and the necklace I bought her, but rarely wears. We went into the bar area.

"Hi. I booked a table for two under the name of Avery?"

The waitress led us to a table which was fairly secluded, to be honest, there were not too many people around as it was still early in the evening.

"How are the boys?" I asked.

"Fine. I've told them that you need to work this weekend, so that lets you off the hook, and that you'd see them next week."

So that puts me back on the hook then, I thought.

We ordered food and drink from the returning waitress. Sauvignon Blanc for Bella, 'Poacher's' for me, Halibut for Bella and King Bill Burger for me.

The conversations which followed were a mixture of anxiety, tenseness, perceived threats, explanation from my part, rebuttals from her part and a battle for any territory.

"Where do you want to start?" Bella said from her legal framework.

"Manchester? When I got the job, you said you would come with me."

"You know fully well why that couldn't happen. I explained it to you at the time and you agreed." Did I? She went on. "The boys schooling, my parent's health, my job," then she added for more emphasis, "or is your job more important than mine?"

Time for the defence counsel. "We had sat at the dining table, and I answered all those questions before I accepted the post."

"Those issues were all left unresolved," she said.

"We went to Manchester, when David and Anna invited us, to take a good look round and you put obstacles in the way all the time. They offered to let us visit anytime to get a better perspective and you never arranged anything."

"If you remember, the boys had started their new school year then."

That was a complete red herring, wasn't it?

Time for some home truths. "Look, I've been really down for a long time, Bella. When I reach out for you, you never seem to warm to me."

"Oh, this is what's really all about, isn't it? Sex."

Actually, it wasn't just that. I was trying to say things like, when I was unhappy at the college she wasn't supportive, she never showed any interest in my work, she blamed me if I tried to do any home improvements and they didn't meet her approval, if I had suggested a way of dealing with the boys and she didn't like it, we had to do it her way. Where do I stop? But now she's come to mention it.

"Well, yes, that too."

She reached under the table and grabbed my cock, shook it from side to side and said in that horrible hissing voice. "It's all about this, isn't it? You'd be happy if we got in the back of your car, and you can fuck me like some sex slave."

That thought had crossed my mind I'll be honest. "Halibut?" said the waitress from behind Bella's back.

After a quick bit of composure, Bella said, "Er, that's mine, thank you."

I wanted to laugh at the incredulity of the timing, but I noticed that Bella wasn't in any laughing mood.

"King Bill Burger," the waitress said as she placed it in front of me. "Can I get you anything else?"

What was she suggesting, a bed?

"No thanks," we both said simultaneously.

Over dinner I tried to find some middle ground and explained that I had done some research (actually, I hadn't, but remembered something that John told me when he and Maria were going through a bad spell) about relationships. If you can remove the sexual element temporarily and concentrate on just the relationship, such as friendliness, co-operation, care, trust, consideration and mutual interests then it would help to raise the awareness of 'wanting' each other again. I couldn't remember what John said it was called so I said.

"I think it's called the Johnson and Johnson technique."

She laughed. "They make talcum powder. It's Masters and Johnson, you mean." She continued laughing at my faux pas. I thought, that's bloody typical, I make a mistake and she finds it hilarious. Great.

Anyway, I explained that if we were apart for a while, that absence will make the heart grow fonder. She countered that with, "Out of sight, out of mind more like."

John had thought that the Masters and Johnson technique was a load of American rubbish, and it was a load of bollocks. I had sown a seed though, and she agreed to think about it.

For an hour or so we talked about other things; the boys schooling, her Choral Society, her parents, the decorators and anything else that would not be contentious as we seemed to have mellowed.

Surprisingly, she agreed that I could come back next Saturday and take the boys out somewhere and we can talk again before I go back to Manchester. I wondered if The

Imps would be playing football at Sincil Bank next week. If not, I could always see if Gainsborough Trinity are playing at home, then John can come too as Sandra is working.

It was strange to watch Bella driving away on her own from the King William car park. I will be honest here; I was so relieved and felt free for the first time in a long time. It was probably unfair to suggest to Bella that there may be light at the end of the tunnel knowing full well it was highly unlikely we'd be back together. I started to wonder when the last time was I fucked her, it didn't really matter.

***

Back at John and Sandra's place, John asked how it went.

"Better than I expected, but there will be more bullets to dodge later, no doubt."

It was now a good time to open some bottles of 'Poacher's' and let the rest of the evening drift into the night. Sandra wasn't averse to 'Poacher's' either and the three of us eventually turned in at about one a.m. As I lay in bed, I realised I hadn't contacted Anna. In my semi-drunken state laying in the dark, I simply texted.

Mission accomplished. Returning to base eleven hundred hours. XXX

I had no idea why I made a military reference, but I needed to put Anna's mind at rest.

Actually, it was nearer twelve noon when we surfaced from our drunken night. I thanked Sandra and John for everything, and we agreed to meet up again soon, possibly next week after I've seen the boys and I am making my way back to Manchester. I never had a sibling, over the twenty-five or so years we have known each other, John has been like a brother to me

***

Back on the road I phoned Anna and gave her a resume of what happened last night, and she sounded so relieved that Bella wasn't too traumatised.

"Did you mention me to her?" Anna said.

"No. Now is not the right time as there is so much other stuff to deal with. I think if she knew about us the shock may be too great."

"Yes, you're probably right."

We agreed I would go and stay in the flat tonight, but I would come for dinner tomorrow and stay over in my old attic room. The girls will need time to take all this in and adjust to all that had happened since the summer.

***

During the Structural Design 1 lecture, I needed the students to recognise the safety factors that are incorporated in the use of structures.

"If you tried to design an aircraft using the same safety factors used in buildings, it would never take off, it would probably be far too heavy. As structural engineers we work out the anticipated dead load (the permanent weight of the structure) then increase it by forty percent. Similarly, live loads (the weight of occupants, furniture, etc.) are worse, they are increased by sixty percent. Then further still, we do not design to the capacity of a material's elastic yield strength but probably only about eighty percent of that value. Can anyone suggest why?"

A lad on the fourth of fifth row volunteered an answer. "To ensure that we never have a failure if loads are accidentally increased?"

"Absolutely."

I then told them of a catastrophic failure that occurred in Kuala Lumpur when a six-storey office building collapsed two years after it was completed. Fortunately, it fell on a Saturday when virtually unoccupied, apart from a few shop workers on the ground floor. Over the two years people who were in the building reported hearing a sound like a whip being cracked occasionally but nobody could identify the source of the sound. Buildings rarely collapse without warning, and this was the same. When the investigators presented their findings eighteen months later, it was shocking to see that decisions had been made about the structure and alterations without consultation with the engineers. Between them, the architect and the client had removed some load bearing columns from the basement, changed the cladding to marble instead of lightweight concrete panels, incorporated a twelve thousand litre water tank on the roof and removed three beams to allow sky lights to be added. The investigation found that there was one particular column that was expected to take a thirteen percent extra load without having any of those other safety factors applied at all.

I always think students respond well if they are exposed to sensationalism.

For greater emphasis, I added. "I was once asked by a chap what I did, I replied I was a structural engineer and he said, 'Oh, you guys, you know that 2 and 2 is four but you'll call it nine for safety'."

That was met with laughter but also an appreciation of the import of their studies.

***

On the way to see Anna I reflected on this. Do we put too much pressure on ourselves to the point where we crack irrevocably?

Now I felt a warm glow inside as I rang the bell and turned the key.

"Are there any munchkins in the vicinity?" I called out.

This time Jasmine and Imogen ran together to greet me. I picked them up, one in each arm and said, "Caught them, now what shall we do with these little munchkins?"

Anna stood framed in the doorway of the kitchen leaning on the frame with her arms folded and smiling sweetly.

"Welcome home," she said. I appreciated the way she had used the word 'home'. At that moment everything became crystal clear, I was, indeed, home.